Processes of Cons
Decisionmaking

2022 Supplement

2022 Supplement
Processes of Constitutional Decisionmaking
Cases and Materials

Eighth Edition

Prepared by Jack M. Balkin

Sanford Levinson
W. St. John Garwood & W. St. John Garwood, Jr. Centennial Chair in Law
University of Texas Law School

Jack M. Balkin
Knight Professor of Constitutional Law and the First Amendment
Yale Law School

Akhil Reed Amar
Sterling Professor of Law and Political Science
Yale Law School

Reva B. Siegel
Nicholas deB. Katzenbach Professor of Law
Yale Law School

Cristina M. Rodríguez
Leighton Homer Surbeck Professor Of Law
Yale Law School

To contact Customer Service, e-mail customer.service@aspenpublishing.com, call 1-800-950-5259, or mail correspondence to:

Aspen Publishing
Attn: Order Department
PO Box 990
Frederick, MD 21705

Printed in the United States of America.

1 2 3 4 5 6 7 8 9 0

ISBN 978-1-5438-5817-4

SUSTAINABLE FORESTRY INITIATIVE

Certified Chain of Custody
At Least Certified Forest Content
www.sfiprogram.org
SFI-01028

About Aspen Publishing

Aspen Publishing is a leading provider of educational content and digital learning solutions to law schools in the U.S. and around the world. Aspen provides best-in-class solutions for legal education through authoritative textbooks, written by renowned authors, and breakthrough products such as Connected eBooks, Connected Quizzing, and PracticePerfect.

The Aspen Casebook Series (famously known among law faculty and students as the "red and black" casebooks) encompasses hundreds of highly regarded textbooks in more than eighty disciplines, from large enrollment courses, such as Torts and Contracts to emerging electives such as Sustainability and the Law of Policing. Study aids such as the *Examples & Explanations* and the *Emanuel Law Outlines* series, both highly popular collections, help law students master complex subject matter.

Major products, programs, and initiatives include:

- **Connected eBooks** are enhanced digital textbooks and study aids that come with a suite of online content and learning tools designed to maximize student success. Designed in collaboration with hundreds of faculty and students, the Connected eBook is a significant leap forward in the legal education learning tools available to students.

- **Connected Quizzing** is an easy-to-use formative assessment tool that tests law students' understanding and provides timely feedback to improve learning outcomes. Delivered through CasebookConnect.com, the learning platform already used by students to access their Aspen casebooks, Connected Quizzing is simple to implement and integrates seamlessly with law school course curricula.

- **PracticePerfect** is a visually engaging, interactive study aid to explain commonly encountered legal doctrines through easy-to-understand animated videos, illustrative examples, and numerous practice questions. Developed by a team of experts, PracticePerfect is the ideal study companion for today's law students.

- The **Aspen Learning Library** enables law schools to provide their students with access to the most popular study aids on the market across all of their courses. Available through an annual subscription, the online library consists of study aids in e-book, audio, and video formats with full text search, note-taking, and highlighting capabilities.

- Aspen's **Digital Bookshelf** is an institutional-level online education bookshelf, consolidating everything students and professors need to ensure success. This program ensures that every student has access to affordable course materials from day one.

- **Leading Edge** is a community centered on thinking differently about legal education and putting those thoughts into actionable strategies. At the core of the program is the Leading Edge Conference, an annual gathering of legal education thought leaders looking to pool ideas and identify promising directions of exploration.

Contents

Processes of Constitutional Decisionmaking

2022 Supplement

Chapter 5

The New Deal and the Civil Rights Era

Insert on p. 600 following Note 5:

UNITED STATES V. VAELLO MADERO, 142 S.Ct. 1539 (2022): Though its powers under the Territory Clause, Congress has created a differential system of taxation and benefits for Puerto Rico. Residents of Puerto Rico are typically exempt from most federal income, gift, estate, and excise taxes. At the same time, the Supplemental Security Income (SSI) program provides benefits only to residents of the 50 States and the District of Columbia. Respondent Vaello Madero had been collecting SSI disability benefits while a resident of New York. He subsequently moved to Puerto Rico and the government sued for repayment of SSI benefits he collected while he resided there. Vaello Madero argued that Congress's decision not to allow Puerto Rican residents to collect SSI benefits violated the equal protection component of the Fifth Amendment's Due Process Clause.

By a vote of 8-1, the Supreme Court, in an opinion by Justice Kavanaugh, reversed the lower court and held that the government had not violated the Fifth Amendment: "Puerto Rico's *tax* status—in particular, the fact that residents of Puerto Rico are typically exempt from most federal income, gift, estate, and excise taxes—supplies a rational basis for likewise distinguishing residents of Puerto Rico from residents of the States for purposes of the Supplemental Security Income *benefits* program. In devising tax and benefits programs, it is reasonable for Congress to take account of the general balance of benefits to and burdens on the residents of Puerto Rico. In doing so, Congress need not conduct a dollar-to-dollar comparison of how its tax and benefits programs apply in the States as compared to the Territories, either at the individual or collective level. Congress need only have a rational basis for its tax and benefits programs. Congress has satisfied that requirement here."

Justice Thomas concurred: "I join the opinion of the Court. I write separately to address the premise that the Due Process Clause of the Fifth Amendment contains an equal protection component whose substance is 'precisely the same' as the Equal Protection Clause of the Fourteenth Amendment. Although I have joined the Court in applying this doctrine, see *Adarand Constructors, Inc. v. Peña*, 515 U.S. 200, 213-217 (1995), I now doubt whether it comports with the original meaning of the Constitution. Firmer ground for prohibiting the Federal Government from discriminating on the basis of race, at least with respect to civil rights, may well be found in the Fourteenth Amendment's Citizenship Clause."

Justice Gorsuch concurred: "A century ago in the Insular Cases, this Court held that the federal government could rule Puerto Rico and other Territories largely without regard to the Constitution. It is past time to acknowledge the gravity of this error and admit what we know to be true: The Insular Cases have no foundation in the Constitution and rest instead on racial stereotypes. They deserve no place in our law. . . . [However,] [b]ecause no party asks us to over-rule the Insular Cases to resolve today's dispute, I join the Court's opinion."

Justice Sotomayor dissented: "there is no rational basis for Congress to treat needy citizens living anywhere in the United States so differently from others. To hold otherwise, as the Court does, is irrational and antithetical to the very nature of the SSI program and the equal protection of citizens guaranteed by the Constitution."

Chapter 6

Federalism, Separation of Powers, and National Security in the Modern Era

Insert on p. 924 before Section B:

TRUMP V. THOMPSON, 142 S.Ct. 680 (2022): [The Select Committee investigating the January 6th attack on the Capitol sent a request to the Archivist of the United States under the Presidential Records Act, 44 U.S.C. § 2205(2)(C), seeking the expeditious disclosure of presidential records pertaining to the events of January 6th, the former President's claims of election fraud in the 2020 presidential election, and other related documents. Former President Trump sought to prevent the Archivist from handing over the documents, claiming executive privilege.

President Biden, applying regulations adopted by the Trump Administration, concluded that a claim of executive privilege as to the documents at issue here was "not in the best interests of the United States," given the "unique and extraordinary circumstances" giving rise to the Committee's request, and Congress's "compelling need" to investigate "an unprecedented effort to obstruct the peaceful transfer of power" and "the most serious attack on the operations of the Federal Government since the Civil War."

Former President Trump then sought a preliminary injunction in the District Court for the District of Columbia, which rejected his request. On appeal, the D.C. Circuit affirmed, holding that "the former President has failed to establish a likelihood of success given (1) President Biden's carefully reasoned and cabined determination that a claim of executive privilege is not in the interests of the United States; (2) Congress's uniquely vital interest in studying the January 6th attack on itself to formulate remedial legislation and to safeguard its constitutional and legislative operations; (3) the demonstrated relevance of the documents at issue to the congressional inquiry; (4) the absence of any identified alternative source for the information; and (5) Mr. Trump's failure even to allege, let alone demonstrate, any particularized harm that would arise from disclosure, any distinct and superseding interest in confidentiality attached to these particular documents, lack of relevance, or any other reasoned justification for withholding the documents. Former President Trump likewise has failed to establish irreparable harm, and the balance of interests and equities weigh decisively in favor of disclosure."

Former President Trump then appealed to the Supreme Court for a stay of the mandate and a preliminary injunction against disclosure of the materials. The Supreme Court denied the request:]

The application for stay of mandate and injunction pending review presented to The Chief Justice and by him referred to the Court is denied. The questions whether and in what circumstances a former President may obtain a court order preventing disclosure of privileged records from his tenure in office, in the face of a determination by the incumbent President to waive the privilege, are unprecedented and raise serious and substantial concerns. The Court of Appeals, however, had no occasion to decide these questions because it analyzed and rejected President Trump's privilege claims "under any of the tests [he] advocated," *Trump v. Thompson*, 20 F.4th 10, 33 (C.A.D.C. 2021), without regard to his status as a former President, *id.*, at 40-46. Because the Court of Appeals concluded that President Trump's claims would have failed even if he were the incumbent, his status as a former President necessarily made no difference to the court's decision. *Id.*, at 33 (noting no "need [to] conclusively resolve whether and to what extent a court," at a former President's behest, may "second guess the sitting President's" decision to release privileged documents); see also *id.*, at 17 n.2. Any discussion of the Court of Appeals concerning President Trump's status as a former President must therefore be regarded as nonbinding dicta.

Justice THOMAS would grant the application.

Statement of Justice KAVANAUGH respecting denial of application.

The Court of Appeals suggested that a former President may not successfully invoke the Presidential communications privilege for communications that occurred during his Presidency, at least if the current President does not support the privilege claim. . . . I respectfully disagree with the Court of Appeals on that point. A former President must be able to successfully invoke the Presidential communications privilege for communications that occurred during his Presidency, even if the current President does not support the privilege claim. Concluding otherwise would eviscerate the executive privilege for Presidential communications. . . .

If Presidents and their advisers thought that the privilege's protections would terminate at the end of the Presidency and that their privileged communications could be disclosed when the President left office (or were subject to the absolute control of a subsequent President who could be a political opponent of a former President), the consequences for the Presidency would be severe. Without sufficient assurances of *continuing* confidentiality, Presidents and their advisers would be chilled from engaging in the full and frank deliberations upon which effective discharge of the President's duties depends.

To be clear, to say that a former President can invoke the privilege for Presidential communications that occurred during his Presidency does not mean that the privilege is absolute or cannot be overcome. The tests set forth in *Nixon*, and *Senate Select Committee on Presidential Campaign Activities v. Nixon*, 498 F.2d 725, 731 (C.A.D.C. 1974) (en banc), may apply to a former President's privilege claim as they do to a current President's privilege claim. Moreover, it could be argued that the strength of a privilege claim should diminish to some extent as the years pass after a former President's term in office. In all events, the *Nixon* and *Senate Select Committee* tests would provide substantial protection for Presidential communications, while still requiring disclosure in certain circumstances.

The Court of Appeals concluded that the privilege claim at issue here would not succeed even under the *Nixon* and *Senate Select Committee* tests. Therefore, as this Court's order today makes clear, the Court of Appeals' broader statements questioning whether a former President may successfully invoke the Presidential communications privilege if the current President does not support the claim were dicta and should not be considered binding precedent going forward.

Chapter 9

Liberty, Equality, and Fundamental Rights: The Constitution, the Family, and the Body

Insert on p. 1582 before Section IV:

DOBBS v. JACKSON WOMEN'S HEALTH ORGANIZATION
142 S.Ct. 2228 (2022)

[Mississippi prohibited performing abortions "[e]xcept in a medical emergency or in the case of a severe fetal abnormality . . . if the probable gestational age of the unborn human being has been determined to be greater than fifteen (15) weeks," a period earlier than viability. The Supreme Court granted certiorari to decide whether to overrule *Roe* and *Casey*.]

Justice ALITO delivered the opinion of the Court.

Abortion presents a profound moral issue on which Americans hold sharply conflicting views. Some believe fervently that a human person comes into being at conception and that abortion ends an innocent life. Others feel just as strongly that any regulation of abortion invades a woman's right to control her own body and prevents women from achieving full equality. Still others in a third group think that abortion should be allowed under some but not all circumstances, and those within this group hold a variety of views about the particular restrictions that should be imposed.

For the first 185 years after the adoption of the Constitution, each State was permitted to address this issue in accordance with the views of its citizens. Then, in 1973, this Court decided *Roe v. Wade*, 410 U.S. 113. Even though the Constitution makes no mention of abortion, the Court held that it confers a broad right to obtain one. It did not claim that American law or the common law had ever recognized such a right, and its survey of history ranged from the constitutionally irrelevant (*e.g.*, its discussion of abortion in antiquity) to the plainly incorrect (*e.g.*, its assertion that abortion was probably never a crime under the common law). After cataloging a wealth of other information having no bearing on the meaning of the Constitution, the opinion concluded with a numbered set of rules much like those that might be found in a statute enacted by a legislature.

Under this scheme, each trimester of pregnancy was regulated differently, but the most critical line was drawn at roughly the end of the second trimester, which, at the time, corresponded to the point at which a fetus was thought to achieve "viability," *i.e.*, the ability to survive outside the womb. Although the Court acknowledged that States had a legitimate interest in protecting "potential life," it found that this interest could not justify any restriction on pre-viability abortions. The Court did not explain the basis for this line, and even abortion supporters have found it hard to defend *Roe*'s reasoning. One prominent constitutional scholar wrote that he "would vote for a statute very much like the one the Court end[ed] up drafting" if he were "a legislator," but his assessment of *Roe* was memorable and brutal: *Roe* was "not constitutional law" at all and gave "almost no sense of an obligation to try to be." [citing John Hart Ely, The Wages of Crying Wolf: A Comment on *Roe v. Wade*, 82 Yale L.J. 920, 926, 947 (1973).]

At the time of *Roe*, 30 States still prohibited abortion at all stages. In the years prior to that decision, about a third of the States had liberalized their laws, but *Roe* abruptly ended that political process. It imposed the same highly restrictive regime on the entire Nation, and it effectively struck down the abortion laws of every single State. As Justice Byron White aptly put it in his dissent, the decision represented the "exercise of raw judicial power," and it sparked a national controversy that has embittered our political culture for a half century.

Eventually, in *Planned Parenthood of Southeastern Pa. v. Casey*, 505 U.S. 833 (1992), the Court revisited *Roe*, but the Members of the Court split three ways. Two Justices expressed no desire to change *Roe* in any way. Four others wanted to overrule the decision in its entirety. And the three remaining Justices, who jointly signed the controlling opinion, took a third position. Their opinion did not endorse *Roe*'s reasoning, and it even hinted that one or more of its authors might have "reservations" about whether the Constitution protects a right to abortion. But the opinion concluded that *stare decisis*, which calls for prior decisions to be followed in most instances, required adherence to what it called *Roe*'s "central holding"—that a State may not constitutionally protect fetal life before "viability"—even if that holding was wrong. Anything less, the opinion claimed, would undermine respect for this Court and the rule of law.

Paradoxically, the judgment in *Casey* did a fair amount of overruling. Several important abortion decisions were overruled *in toto*, and *Roe* itself was overruled in part. *Casey* threw out *Roe*'s trimester scheme and substituted a new rule of uncertain origin under which States were forbidden to adopt any regulation that imposed an "undue burden" on a woman's right to have an abortion. The decision provided no clear guidance about the difference between a "due" and an "undue" burden. But the three Justices who authored the controlling opinion "call[ed] the contending sides of a national controversy to end their national division" by treating the Court's decision as the final settlement of the question of the constitutional right to abortion.

As has become increasingly apparent in the intervening years, *Casey* did not achieve that goal. Americans continue to hold passionate and widely divergent views on abortion, and state legislatures have acted accordingly. Some have recently enacted laws allowing abortion, with few restrictions, at all stages of pregnancy. Others have tightly restricted abortion beginning well before viability.

And in this case, 26 States have expressly asked this Court to overrule *Roe* and *Casey* and allow the States to regulate or prohibit pre-viability abortions. . . .

We hold that *Roe* and *Casey* must be overruled. The Constitution makes no reference to abortion, and no such right is implicitly protected by any constitutional provision, including the one on which the defenders of *Roe* and *Casey* now chiefly rely—the Due Process Clause of the Fourteenth Amendment. That provision has been held to guarantee some rights that are not mentioned in the Constitution, but any such right must be "deeply rooted in this Nation's history and tradition" and "implicit in the concept of ordered liberty." *Washington v. Glucksberg,* 521 U.S. 702, 721 (1997) (internal quotation marks omitted).

The right to abortion does not fall within this category. Until the latter part of the 20th century, such a right was entirely unknown in American law. Indeed, when the Fourteenth Amendment was adopted, three quarters of the States made abortion a crime at all stages of pregnancy. The abortion right is also critically different from any other right that this Court has held to fall within the Fourteenth Amendment's protection of "liberty." *Roe*'s defenders characterize the abortion right as similar to the rights recognized in past decisions involving matters such as intimate sexual relations, contraception, and marriage, but abortion is fundamentally different, as both *Roe* and *Casey* acknowledged, because it destroys what those decisions called "fetal life" and what the law now before us describes as an "unborn human being."

Stare decisis, the doctrine on which *Casey*'s controlling opinion was based, does not compel unending adherence to *Roe*'s abuse of judicial authority. *Roe* was egregiously wrong from the start. Its reasoning was exceptionally weak, and the decision has had damaging consequences. And far from bringing about a national settlement of the abortion issue, *Roe* and *Casey* have enflamed debate and deepened division.

It is time to heed the Constitution and return the issue of abortion to the people's elected representatives. "The permissibility of abortion, and the limitations, upon it, are to be resolved like most important questions in our democracy: by citizens trying to persuade one another and then voting." *Casey,* 505 U. S., at 979 (Scalia, J., concurring in judgment in part and dissenting in part). That is what the Constitution and the rule of law demand.

. . . .

II

We begin by considering the critical question whether the Constitution, properly understood, confers a right to obtain an abortion. Skipping over that question, the controlling opinion in *Casey* reaffirmed *Roe*'s "central holding" based solely on the doctrine of *stare decisis,* but as we will explain, proper application of *stare decisis* required an assessment of the strength of the grounds on which *Roe* was based.

We therefore turn to the question that the *Casey* plurality did not consider, and we address that question in three steps. First, we explain the standard that our cases have used in determining whether the Fourteenth Amendment's reference to "liberty" protects a particular right. Second, we examine whether the right at issue in this case is rooted in our Nation's history and tradition and whether it is an essential component of what we have described as "ordered liberty." Finally, we consider whether a right to obtain an abortion is part of a broader entrenched right that is supported by other precedents.

A

Constitutional analysis must begin with "the language of the instrument.". . . . The Constitution makes no express reference to a right to obtain an abortion, and therefore those who claim that it protects such a right must show that the right is somehow implicit in the constitutional text.

Roe, however, was remarkably loose in its treatment of the constitutional text. It held that the abortion right, which is not mentioned in the Constitution, is part of a right to privacy, which is also not mentioned. And that privacy right, *Roe* observed, had been found to spring from no fewer than five different constitutional provisions—the First, Fourth, Fifth, Ninth, and Fourteenth Amendments. . . . *Roe* expressed the "feel[ing]" that the Fourteenth Amendment was the provision that did the work, but its message seemed to be that the abortion right could be found *somewhere* in the Constitution and that specifying its exact location was not of paramount importance. The *Casey* Court did not defend this unfocused analysis and instead grounded its decision solely on the theory that the right to obtain an abortion is part of the "liberty" protected by the Fourteenth Amendment's Due Process Clause.

[S]ome of respondents' *amici* have now offered . . . yet another potential home for the abortion right: the Fourteenth Amendment's Equal Protection Clause. Neither *Roe* nor *Casey* saw fit to invoke this theory, and it is squarely foreclosed by our precedents, which establish that a State's regulation of abortion is not a sex-based classification and is thus not subject to the "heightened scrutiny" that applies to such classifications. The regulation of a medical procedure that only one sex can undergo does not trigger heightened constitutional scrutiny unless the regulation is a "mere pretex[t] designed to effect an invidious discrimination against members of one sex or the other." *Geduldig v. Aiello*, 417 U.S. 484, 496, n. 20 (1974). And as the Court has stated, the "goal of preventing abortion" does not constitute "invidiously discriminatory animus" against women. *Bray v. Alexandria Women's Health Clinic*, 506 U.S. 263, 273-274 (1993) (internal quotation marks omitted). Accordingly, laws regulating or prohibiting abortion are not subject to heightened scrutiny. Rather, they are governed by the same standard of review as other health and safety measures. . . .

With this new theory addressed, we turn to *Casey*'s bold assertion that the abortion right is an aspect of the "liberty" protected by the Due Process Clause of the Fourteenth Amendment.

The underlying theory on which this argument rests—that the Fourteenth Amendment's Due Process Clause provides substantive, as well as procedural, protection for "liberty"—has long been controversial. But our decisions have held that the Due Process Clause protects two categories of substantive rights.

The first consists of rights guaranteed by the first eight Amendments. . . .[T]his Court has held that the Due Process Clause of the Fourteenth Amendment "incorporates" the great majority of those rights and thus makes them equally applicable to the States. The second category — which is the one in question here — comprises a select list of fundamental rights that are not mentioned anywhere in the Constitution.

In deciding whether a right falls into either of these categories, the Court has long asked whether the right is "deeply rooted in [our] history and tradition" and whether it is essential to our Nation's "scheme of ordered liberty." *Timbs v. Indiana*, 586 U.S. ___, ___ (2019) (slip op., at 3) (internal quotation marks omitted); *McDonald* [*v. Chicago*, 561 U. S., 742, 764, 767 (2010)] (internal quotation marks omitted); [*Washington v.*] *Glucksberg*, 521 U.S. 702, 721 (1997) (internal quotation marks omitted). And in conducting this inquiry, we have engaged in a careful analysis of the history of the right at issue. . . . [I]n *Glucksberg*, which held that the Due Process Clause does not confer a right to assisted suicide, the Court surveyed more than 700 years of "Anglo-American common law tradition," and made clear that a fundamental right must be "objectively, deeply rooted in this Nation's history and tradition."

Historical inquiries of this nature are essential whenever we are asked to recognize a new component of the "liberty" protected by the Due Process Clause because the term "liberty" alone provides little guidance. "Liberty" is a capacious term. As Lincoln once said: "We all declare for Liberty; but in using the same word we do not all mean the same thing." In a well-known essay, Isaiah Berlin reported that "[h]istorians of ideas" had cataloged more than 200 different senses in which the term had been used.

In interpreting what is meant by the Fourteenth Amendment's reference to "liberty," we must guard against the natural human tendency to confuse what that Amendment protects with our own ardent views about the liberty that Americans should enjoy. That is why the Court has long been "reluctant" to recognize rights that are not mentioned in the Constitution. . . . As the Court cautioned in *Glucksberg*, "[w]e must . . . exercise the utmost care whenever we are asked to break new ground in this field, lest the liberty protected by the Due Process Clause be subtly transformed into the policy preferences of the Members of this Court."

On occasion, when the Court has ignored the "[a]ppropriate limits" imposed by " 'respect for the teachings of history,' " *Moore,* 431 U. S., at 503 (plurality opinion), it has fallen into the freewheeling judicial policymaking that characterized discredited decisions such as *Lochner v. New York*, 198 U.S. 45 (1905). The Court must not fall prey to such an unprincipled approach. Instead, guided by the history and tradition that map the essential components of our Nation's concept of ordered liberty, we must ask what the *Fourteenth Amendment* means by the term "liberty." When we engage in that inquiry in the present case, the clear answer is that the Fourteenth Amendment does not protect the right to an abortion.

. . . That is true regardless of whether we look to the Amendment's Due Process Clause or its Privileges or Immunities Clause. Some scholars and

Justices have maintained that the Privileges or Immunities Clause is the provision of the Fourteenth Amendment that guarantees substantive rights. But even on that view, such a right would need to be rooted in the Nation's history and tradition. See *Corfield v. Coryell*, 6 F. Cas. 546, 551-552 (No. 3,230) (CC ED Pa. 1823) (describing unenumerated rights under the Privileges and Immunities Clause, Art. IV, § 2, as those "fundamental" rights "which have, at all times, been enjoyed by the citizens of the several states"). [relocated footnote—eds.]

B

1

Until the latter part of the 20th century, there was no support in American law for a constitutional right to obtain an abortion. No state constitutional provision had recognized such a right. Until a few years before *Roe* was handed down, no federal or state court had recognized such a right. Nor had any scholarly treatise of which we are aware. And although law review articles are not reticent about advocating new rights, the earliest article proposing a constitutional right to abortion that has come to our attention was published only a few years before *Roe*.

Not only was there no support for such a constitutional right until shortly before *Roe*, but abortion had long been a *crime* in every single State. At common law, abortion was criminal in at least some stages of pregnancy and was regarded as unlawful and could have very serious consequences at all stages. American law followed the common law until a wave of statutory restrictions in the 1800s expanded criminal liability for abortions. By the time of the adoption of the Fourteenth Amendment, three-quarters of the States had made abortion a crime at any stage of pregnancy, and the remaining States would soon follow.

Roe either ignored or misstated this history, and *Casey* declined to reconsider *Roe*'s faulty historical analysis. It is therefore important to set the record straight.

2

We begin with the common law, under which abortion was a crime at least after "quickening"—*i.e.*, the first felt movement of the fetus in the womb, which usually occurs between the 16th and 18th week of pregnancy. The "eminent common-law authorities (Blackstone, Coke, Hale, and the like)," *all* describe abortion after quickening as criminal. Henry de Bracton's 13th-century treatise explained that if a person has "struck a pregnant woman, or has given her poison, whereby he has caused abortion, if the foetus be already formed and animated, and particularly if it be animated, he commits homicide." 2 De Legibus et Consuetudinibus Angliae 279 (T. Twiss ed. 1879); see also 1 Fleta, c. 23, reprinted in 72 Selden Soc. 60-61 (H. Richardson & G. Sayles eds. 1955) (13th-century treatise). Sir Edward Coke's 17th-century treatise likewise asserted that abortion of a quick child was "murder" if the "childe be born alive" and a "great misprision" if the "childe dieth in her body." 3 Institutes of the Laws of England

50-51 (1644). ("Misprision" referred to "some heynous offence under the degree of felony.") Two treatises by Sir Matthew Hale likewise described abortion of a quick child who died in the womb as a "great crime" and a "great misprision." Pleas of the Crown 53 (P. Glazebrook ed. 1972); 1 History of the Pleas of the Crown 433 (1736) (Hale). And writing near the time of the adoption of our Constitution, William Blackstone explained that abortion of a "quick" child was "by the ancient law homicide or manslaughter" (citing Bracton), and at least a very "heinous misdemeanor" (citing Coke). 1 Commentaries on the Laws of England 129-130 (7th ed. 1775) (Blackstone). English cases dating all the way back to the 13th century corroborate the treatises' statements that abortion was a crime. . . . In 1732, for example, Eleanor Beare was convicted of "destroying the Foetus in the Womb" of another woman and "thereby causing her to miscarry." For that crime and another "misdemeanor," Beare was sentenced to two days in the pillory and three years' imprisonment.

Although a pre-quickening abortion was not itself considered homicide, it does not follow that abortion was *permissible* at common law—much less that abortion was a legal *right*. Quite to the contrary, in the 1732 case mentioned above, the judge said of the charge of abortion (with no mention of quickening) that he had "never met with a case so barbarous and unnatural." Similarly, an indictment from 1602, which did not distinguish between a pre-quickening and post-quickening abortion, described abortion as "pernicious" and "against the peace of our Lady the Queen, her crown and dignity."

That the common law did not condone even prequickening abortions is confirmed by what one might call a proto-felony-murder rule. Hale and Blackstone explained a way in which a pre-quickening abortion could rise to the level of a homicide. Hale wrote that if a physician gave a woman "with child" a "potion" to cause an abortion, and the woman died, it was "murder" because the potion was given "*unlawfully* to destroy her child within her." 1 Hale 429-430 (emphasis added). . . . . In sum, although common-law authorities differed on the severity of punishment for abortions committed at different points in pregnancy, none endorsed the practice. Moreover, we are aware of no common-law case or authority, and the parties have not pointed to any, that remotely suggests a positive *right* to procure an abortion at any stage of pregnancy.

In this country, the historical record is similar. The "most important early American edition of Blackstone's Commentaries," reported Blackstone's statement that abortion of a quick child was at least "a heinous misdemeanor," 2 St. George Tucker, Blackstone's Commentaries 129-130 (1803), and that edition also included Blackstone's discussion of the proto-felony-murder rule. . . . The few cases available from the early colonial period corroborate that abortion was a crime. . . . And by the 19th century, courts frequently explained that the common law made abortion of a quick child a crime.

The original ground for drawing a distinction between pre- and post-quickening abortions is not entirely clear, but some have attributed the rule to the difficulty of proving that a pre-quickening fetus was alive. At that time, there were no scientific methods for detecting pregnancy in its early stages. . . . The Solicitor General offers a different explanation of the basis for the quickening rule, namely, that before quickening the common law did not regard a fetus "as having a 'separate and independent existence.' " . . . At any rate, the original ground for the quickening rule is of little importance for present purposes because the rule was abandoned in the 19th century. During that period, treatise writers and commentators criticized the quickening distinction as "neither in accordance with the result of medical experience, nor with the principles of the common law." . . . In 1803, the British Parliament made abortion a crime at all stages of pregnancy and authorized the imposition of severe punishment. One scholar has suggested that Parliament's decision "may partly have been attributable to the medical man's concern that fetal life should be protected by the law at all stages of gestation."

In this country during the 19th century, the vast majority of the States enacted statutes criminalizing abortion at all stages of pregnancy. By 1868, the year when the Fourteenth Amendment was ratified, three-quarters of the States, 28 out of 37, had enacted statutes making abortion a crime even if it was performed before quickening. Of the nine States that had not yet criminalized abortion at all stages, all but one did so by 1910. . . . This overwhelming consensus endured until the day *Roe* was decided. At that time, also by the *Roe* Court's own count, a substantial majority — 30 States — still prohibited abortion at all stages except to save the life of the mother. And though *Roe* discerned a "trend toward liberalization" in about "one-third of the States," those States still criminalized some abortions and regulated them more stringently than *Roe* would allow. In short, the "Court's opinion in *Roe* itself convincingly refutes the notion that the abortion liberty is deeply rooted in the history or tradition of our people."

The inescapable conclusion is that a right to abortion is not deeply rooted in the Nation's history and traditions. On the contrary, an unbroken tradition of prohibiting abortion on pain of criminal punishment persisted from the earliest days of the common law until 1973. The Court in *Roe* could have said of abortion exactly what *Glucksberg* said of assisted suicide: "Attitudes toward [abortion] have changed since Bracton, but our laws have consistently condemned, and continue to prohibit, [that practice]."

Respondents and their *amici* have no persuasive answer to this historical evidence.

Neither respondents nor the Solicitor General disputes the fact that by 1868 the vast majority of States criminalized abortion at all stages of pregnancy. Instead, respondents are forced to argue that it "does [not] matter that some States prohibited abortion at the time *Roe* was decided or when the Fourteenth Amendment was adopted." But that argument flies in the face of the standard we have applied in determining whether an asserted right that is nowhere mentioned in the Constitution is nevertheless protected by the Fourteenth Amendment.

Not only are respondents and their *amici* unable to show that a constitutional right to abortion was established when the Fourteenth Amendment was adopted, but they have found no support for the existence of an abortion right that predates the latter part of the 20th century — no state constitutional provision, no statute, no judicial decision, no learned treatise. The earliest sources called to our attention are a few district court and state court decisions decided shortly before *Roe* and a small number of law review articles from the same time period.

A few of respondents' *amici* muster historical arguments, but they are very weak. The Solicitor General repeats *Roe*'s claim that it is " 'doubtful' . . . 'abortion was ever firmly established as a common-law crime even with respect to the destruction of a quick fetus.' " But as we have seen, great common-law authorities like Bracton, Coke, Hale, and Blackstone all wrote that a post-quickening abortion was a crime — and a serious one at that. Moreover, Hale and Blackstone (and many other authorities following them) asserted that even a pre-quickening abortion was "unlawful" and that, as a result, an abortionist was guilty of murder if the woman died from the attempt. . . . .

The Solicitor General next suggests that history supports an abortion right because the common law's failure to criminalize abortion before quickening means that "at the Founding and for decades thereafter, women generally could terminate a pregnancy, at least in its early stages." But the insistence on quickening was not universal, see *Mills v. Commonwealth*, 13 Pa. 631, 633 (1850); *State v. Slagle*, 83 N. C. 630, 632 (1880), and regardless, the fact that many States in the late 18th and early 19th century did not criminalize pre-quickening abortions does not mean that anyone thought the States lacked the authority to do so. When legislatures began to exercise that authority as the century wore on, no one, as far as we are aware, argued that the laws they enacted violated a fundamental right. That is not surprising since common-law authorities had repeatedly condemned abortion and described it as an "unlawful" act without regard to whether it occurred before or after quickening. . . . In any event, *Roe*, *Casey*, and other related abortion decisions imposed substantial restrictions on a State's capacity to regulate abortions performed after quickening. [relocated footnote — eds.]

C

Instead of seriously pressing the argument that the abortion right itself has deep roots, supporters of *Roe* and *Casey* contend that the abortion right is an integral part of a broader entrenched right. *Roe* termed this a right to privacy, and *Casey* described it as the freedom to make "intimate and personal choices" that are "central to personal dignity and autonomy," *Casey* elaborated: "At the heart of liberty is the right to define one's own concept of existence, of meaning, of the universe, and of the mystery of human life."

The Court did not claim that this broadly framed right is absolute, and no such claim would be plausible. . . .

Ordered liberty sets limits and defines the boundary between competing interests. *Roe* and *Casey* each struck a particular balance between the interests of a woman who wants an abortion and the interests of what they termed "potential life." But the people of the various States may evaluate those interests differently. In some States, voters may believe that the abortion right should be even more extensive than the right that *Roe* and *Casey* recognized. Voters in other States may wish to impose tight restrictions based on their belief that abortion destroys an "unborn human being." Miss. Code Ann. § 41-41-191(4)(b). Our Nation's historical understanding of ordered liberty does not prevent the people's elected representatives from deciding how abortion should be regulated.

Nor does the right to obtain an abortion have a sound basis in precedent. *Casey* relied on cases involving the right to marry a person of a different race, *Loving v. Virginia*, 388 U.S. 1 (1967); the right to marry while in prison, *Turner v. Safley*, 482 U.S. 78 (1987); the right to obtain contraceptives, *Griswold v. Connecticut*, 381 U.S. 479 (1965), *Eisenstadt v. Baird*, 405 U.S. 438 (1972), *Carey v. Population Services Int'l*, 431 U.S. 678 (1977); the right to reside with relatives, *Moore v. East Cleveland*, 431 U.S. 494 (1977); the right to make decisions about the education of one's children, *Pierce v. Society of Sisters*, 268 U.S. 510 (1925), *Meyer v. Nebraska*, 262 U.S. 390 (1923); the right not to be sterilized without consent, *Skinner v. Oklahoma ex rel. Williamson*, 316 U.S. 535 (1942); and the right in certain circumstances not to undergo involuntary surgery, forced administration of drugs, or other substantially similar procedures, *Winston v. Lee*, 470 U.S. 753 (1985), *Washington v. Harper*, 494 U.S. 210 (1990), *Rochin v. California*, 342 U.S. 165 (1952). Respondents and the Solicitor General also rely on post-*Casey* decisions like *Lawrence v. Texas*, 539 U.S. 558 (2003) (right to engage in private, consensual sexual acts), and *Obergefell v. Hodges*, 576 U.S. 644 (2015) (right to marry a person of the same sex).

These attempts to justify abortion through appeals to a broader right to autonomy and to define one's "concept of existence" prove too much. *Casey*, 505 U. S., at 851. Those criteria, at a high level of generality, could license fundamental rights to illicit drug use, prostitution, and the like. None of these rights has any claim to being deeply rooted in history.

What sharply distinguishes the abortion right from the rights recognized in the cases on which *Roe* and *Casey* rely is something that both those decisions acknowledged: Abortion destroys what those decisions call "potential life" and what the law at issue in this case regards as the life of an "unborn human being." None of the other decisions cited by *Roe* and *Casey* involved the critical moral question posed by abortion. They are therefore inapposite. They do not support the right to obtain an abortion, and by the same token, our conclusion that the Constitution does not confer such a right does not undermine them in any way.

In drawing this critical distinction between the abortion right and other rights, it is not necessary to dispute *Casey*'s claim (which we accept for the sake of argument) that "the specific practices of States at the time of the adoption of the Fourteenth Amendment" do not "mar[k] the outer limits of the substantive sphere of liberty which the Fourteenth Amendment protects." Abortion is nothing new. It has been addressed by lawmakers for centuries, and the fundamental moral question that it poses is ageless.

Defenders of *Roe* and *Casey* do not claim that any new scientific learning calls for a different answer to the underlying moral question, but they do contend that changes in society require the recognition of a constitutional right to obtain an abortion. Without the availability of abortion, they maintain, people will be inhibited from exercising their freedom to choose the types of relationships they desire, and women will be unable to compete with men in the workplace and in other endeavors.

Americans who believe that abortion should be restricted press countervailing arguments about modern developments. They note that attitudes about the pregnancy of unmarried women have changed drastically; that federal and state laws ban discrimination on the basis of pregnancy; that leave for pregnancy and childbirth are now guaranteed by law in many cases; that the costs of medical care associated with pregnancy are covered by insurance or government assistance; that States have increasingly adopted "safe haven" laws, which generally allow women to drop off babies anonymously; and that a woman who puts her newborn up for adoption today has little reason to fear that the baby will not find a suitable home. They also claim that many people now have a new appreciation of fetal life and that when prospective parents who want to have a child view a sonogram, they typically have no doubt that what they see is their daughter or son.

Both sides make important policy arguments, but supporters of *Roe* and *Casey* must show that this Court has the authority to weigh those arguments and decide how abortion may be regulated in the States. They have failed to make that showing, and we thus return the power to weigh those arguments to the people and their elected representatives.

D

The dissent is very candid that it cannot show that a constitutional right to abortion has any foundation, let alone a " 'deeply rooted' " one, " 'in this Nation's history and tradition.' " The dissent does not identify *any* pre-*Roe* authority that supports such a right—no state constitutional provision or statute, no federal or state judicial precedent, not even a scholarly treatise. Nor does the dissent dispute the fact that abortion was illegal at common law at least after quickening; that the 19th century saw a trend toward criminalization of pre-quickening abortions; that by 1868, a supermajority of States (at least 26 of 37) had enacted statutes criminalizing abortion at all stages of pregnancy; that by the late 1950s at least 46 States prohibited abortion "however and whenever performed" except if necessary to save "the life of the mother;" and that when *Roe* was decided in 1973 similar statutes were still in effect in 30 States. . . . By way of contrast, at the time *Griswold v. Connecticut*, 381 U.S. 479 (1965), was decided, the Connecticut statute at issue was an extreme outlier. [relocated footnote—eds.]

The dissent's failure to engage with this long tradition is devastating to its position. We have held that the "established method of substantive-due-process analysis" requires that an unenumerated right be " 'deeply rooted in this Nation's history and tradition' " before it can be recognized as a component of the "liberty" protected in the Due Process Clause. *Glucksberg*. But despite the dissent's professed fidelity to *stare decisis*, it fails to seriously engage with that important precedent—which it cannot possibly satisfy.

The dissent attempts to obscure this failure by misrepresenting our application of *Glucksberg*. The dissent suggests that we have focused only on "the legal status of abortion in the 19th century," but our review of this Nation's tradition extends well past that period. As explained, for more than a century after 1868—including "another half-century" after women gained the constitutional right to vote in 1920, . . . it was firmly established that laws prohibiting abortion like the Texas law at issue in *Roe* were permissible exercises of state regulatory authority. And today, another half century later, more than half of the States have asked us to overrule *Roe* and *Casey*. The dissent cannot establish that a right to abortion has *ever* been part of this Nation's tradition.

Because the dissent cannot argue that the abortion right is rooted in this Nation's history and tradition, it contends that the "constitutional tradition" is "not captured whole at a single moment," and that its "meaning gains content from the long sweep of our history and from successive judicial precedents." This vague formulation imposes no clear restraints on what Justice White called the "exercise of raw judicial power," and while the dissent claims that its standard "does not mean anything goes," any real restraints are hard to discern.

. . . First, if the "long sweep of history" imposes any restraint on the recognition of unenumerated rights, then *Roe* was surely wrong, since abortion was never allowed (except to save the life of the mother) in a majority of States for over 100 years before that decision was handed down. Second, it is impossible to defend *Roe* based on prior precedent because all of the precedents *Roe* cited, including *Griswold* and *Eisenstadt*, were critically different for a reason that we have explained: None of those cases involved the destruction of what *Roe* called "potential life."

So without support in history or relevant precedent, *Roe*'s reasoning cannot be defended even under the dissent's proposed test, and the dissent is forced to rely solely on the fact that a constitutional right to abortion was recognized in *Roe* and later decisions that accepted *Roe*'s interpretation. . . . But as the Court has reiterated time and time again, adherence to precedent is not " 'an inexorable command.' " There are occasions when past decisions should be overruled, and as we will explain, this is one of them.

The most striking feature of the dissent is the absence of any serious discussion of the legitimacy of the States' interest in protecting fetal life. This is evident in the analogy that the dissent draws between the abortion right and the rights recognized in *Griswold* (contraception), *Eisenstadt* (same), *Lawrence* (sexual conduct with member of the same sex), and *Obergefell* (same-sex marriage). Perhaps this is designed to stoke unfounded fear that our decision will imperil those other rights, but the dissent's analogy is objectionable for a more important reason: what it reveals about the dissent's views on the protection of what *Roe* called "potential life." The exercise of the rights at issue in *Griswold*, *Eisenstadt*, *Lawrence*, and *Obergefell* does not destroy a "potential life," but an abortion has that effect. So if the rights at issue in those cases are fundamentally the same as the right recognized in *Roe* and *Casey*, the implication is clear: The Constitution does not permit the States to regard the destruction of a "potential life" as a matter of any significance.

That view is evident throughout the dissent. The dissent has much to say about the effects of pregnancy on women, the burdens of motherhood, and the difficulties faced by poor women. These are important concerns. However, the dissent evinces no similar regard for a State's interest in protecting prenatal life. The dissent repeatedly praises the "balance," that the viability line strikes between a woman's liberty interest and the State's interest in prenatal life. But . . . . the viability line makes no sense. It was not adequately justified in *Roe*, and the dissent does not even try to defend it today. Nor does it identify any other point in a pregnancy after which a State is permitted to prohibit the destruction of a fetus.

Our opinion is not based on any view about if and when prenatal life is entitled to any of the rights enjoyed after birth. The dissent, by contrast, would impose on the people a particular theory about when the rights of personhood begin. According to the dissent, the Constitution *requires* the States to regard a fetus as lacking even the most basic human right — to live — at least until an arbitrary point in a pregnancy has passed. Nothing in the Constitution or in our Nation's legal traditions authorizes the Court to adopt that " 'theory of life.' "

III

We next consider whether the doctrine of *stare decisis* counsels continued acceptance of *Roe* and *Casey*. *Stare decisis* plays an important role in our case law, and we have explained that it serves many valuable ends. It protects the interests of those who have taken action in reliance on a past decision. It "reduces incentives for challenging settled precedents, saving parties and courts the expense of endless relitigation." It fosters "evenhanded" decisionmaking by requiring that like cases be decided in a like manner. It "contributes to the actual and perceived integrity of the judicial process." And it restrains judicial hubris and reminds us to respect the judgment of those who have grappled with important questions in the past. [But] some of our most important constitutional decisions have overruled prior precedents. [citing as examples *Brown v. Board of Education*, *West Coast Hotel v. Parrish*, and *West Virginia Bd. of Ed. v. Barnette*, 319 U.S. 624 (1943).] On many other occasions, this Court has overruled important constitutional decisions. . . . Without these decisions, American constitutional law as we know it would be unrecognizable, and this would be a different country.

Our cases have attempted to provide a framework for deciding when a precedent should be overruled, and they have identified factors that should be considered in making such a decision.

In this case, five factors weigh strongly in favor of overruling *Roe* and *Casey*: the nature of their error, the quality of their reasoning, the "workability" of the rules they imposed on the country, their disruptive effect on other areas of the law, and the absence of concrete reliance.

A

The nature of the Court's error. An erroneous interpretation of the Constitution is always important, but some are more damaging than others.

The infamous decision in *Plessy v. Ferguson*, was one such decision. . . . It was "egregiously wrong" on the day it was decided. . . . *Roe* was also egregiously wrong and deeply damaging. . . . *Roe*'s constitutional analysis was far outside the bounds of any reasonable interpretation of the various constitutional provisions to which it vaguely pointed.

Roe was on a collision course with the Constitution from the day it was decided, *Casey* perpetuated its errors. . . .[W]ielding nothing but "raw judicial power," *Roe*, 410 U. S., at 222 (White, J., dissenting), the Court usurped the power to address a question of profound moral and social importance that the Constitution unequivocally leaves for the people. *Casey* described itself as calling both sides of the national controversy to resolve their debate, but in doing so, *Casey* necessarily declared a winning side. Those on the losing side — those who sought to advance the State's interest in fetal life — could no longer seek to persuade their elected representatives to adopt policies consistent with their views. The Court short-circuited the democratic process by closing it to the large number of Americans who dissented in any respect from *Roe*. "*Roe* fanned into life an issue that has inflamed our national politics in general, and has obscured with its smoke the selection of Justices to this Court in particular, ever since." *Casey*, 505 U. S., at 995-996 (opinion of Scalia, J.). Together, *Roe* and *Casey* represent an error that cannot be allowed to stand. . . .

B

The quality of the reasoning. . . . *Roe* found that the Constitution implicitly conferred a right to obtain an abortion, but it failed to ground its decision in text, history, or precedent. It relied on an erroneous historical narrative; it devoted great attention to and presumably relied on matters that have no bearing on the meaning of the Constitution; it disregarded the fundamental difference between the precedents on which it relied and the question before the Court; it concocted an elaborate set of rules, with different restrictions for each trimester of pregnancy, but it did not explain how this veritable code could be teased out of anything in the Constitution, the history of abortion laws, prior precedent, or any other cited source; and its most important rule (that States cannot protect fetal life prior to "viability") was never raised by any party and has never been plausibly explained. *Roe*'s reasoning quickly drew scathing scholarly criticism, even from supporters of broad access to abortion.

The *Casey* plurality, while reaffirming *Roe*'s central holding, pointedly refrained from endorsing most of its reasoning. It revised the textual basis for the abortion right, silently abandoned *Roe*'s erroneous historical narrative, and jettisoned the trimester framework. But it replaced that scheme with an arbitrary "undue burden" test and relied on an exceptional version of *stare decisis* that, as explained below, this Court had never before applied and has never invoked since.

The weaknesses in *Roe*'s reasoning are well-known. Without any grounding in the constitutional text, history, or precedent, it imposed on the entire country a detailed set of rules much like those that one might expect to find in a statute or regulation. . . . This elaborate scheme was the Court's own brainchild. Neither party advocated the trimester framework; nor did either party or any *amicus* argue that "viability" should mark the point at which the scope of the abortion right and a State's regulatory authority should be substantially transformed.

Not only did this scheme resemble the work of a legislature, but the Court made little effort to explain how these rules could be deduced from any of the sources on which constitutional decisions are usually based. . . .

Roe featured a lengthy survey of history, but much of its discussion was irrelevant, and the Court made no effort to explain why it was included. . . .When it came to the most important historical fact—how the States regulated abortion when the Fourteenth Amendment was adopted—the Court said almost nothing. It allowed that States had tightened their abortion laws "in the middle and late 19th century," but it implied that these laws might have been enacted not to protect fetal life but to further "a Victorian social concern" about "illicit sexual conduct."

Roe's failure even to note the overwhelming consensus of state laws in effect in 1868 is striking, and what it said about the common law was simply wrong. . . . After surveying history, the opinion spent many paragraphs conducting the sort of fact-finding that might be undertaken by a legislative committee. This included a lengthy account of the "position of the American Medical Association" and "[t]he position of the American Public Health Association," as well as the vote by the American Bar Association's House of Delegates in February 1972 on proposed abortion legislation. Also noted were a British judicial decision handed down in 1939 and a new British abortion law enacted in 1967. The Court did not explain why these sources shed light on the meaning of the Constitution, and not one of them adopted or advocated anything like the scheme that *Roe* imposed on the country.

Finally, after all this, the Court turned to precedent. Citing a broad array of cases, the Court found support for a constitutional "right of personal privacy," but it conflated two very different meanings of the term: the right to shield information from disclosure and the right to make and implement important personal decisions without governmental interference. Only the cases involving this second sense of the term could have any possible relevance to the abortion issue, and some of the cases in that category involved personal decisions that were obviously very, very far afield. See *Pierce*, 268 U.S. 510 (right to send children to religious school); *Meyer*, 262 U.S. 390 (right to have children receive German language instruction).

What remained was a handful of cases having something to do with marriage, *Loving*, 388 U.S. 1 (right to marry a person of a different race), or procreation, *Skinner*, 316 U.S. 535 (right not to be sterilized); *Griswold*, 381 U.S. 479 (right of married persons to obtain contraceptives); *Eisenstadt*, 405 U.S. 438 (same, for unmarried persons). But none of these decisions involved what is distinctive about abortion: its effect on what *Roe* termed "potential life."

When the Court summarized the basis for the scheme it imposed on the country, it asserted that its rules were "consistent with" the following: (1) "the relative weights of the respective interests involved," (2) "the lessons and examples of medical and legal history," (3) "the lenity of the common law," and (4) "the demands of the profound problems of the present day." Put aside the second and third factors, which were based on the Court's flawed account of history, and what remains are precisely the sort of considerations that legislative bodies often take into account when they draw lines that accommodate competing interests. The scheme *Roe* produced *looked* like legislation, and the Court provided the sort of explanation that might be expected from a legislative body.

What *Roe* did not provide was any cogent justification for the lines it drew. Why, for example, does a State have no authority to regulate first trimester abortions for the purpose of protecting a woman's health? The Court's only explanation was that mortality rates for abortion at that stage were lower than the mortality rates for childbirth. But the Court did not explain why mortality rates were the only factor that a State could legitimately consider. Many health and safety regulations aim to avoid adverse health consequences short of death. And the Court did not explain why it departed from the normal rule that courts defer to the judgments of legislatures "in areas fraught with medical and scientific uncertainties."

An even more glaring deficiency was *Roe*'s failure to justify the critical distinction it drew between pre- and post-viability abortions. Here is the Court's entire explanation:

> "With respect to the State's important and legitimate interest in potential life, the 'compelling' point is at viability. This is so because the fetus then presumably has the capability of meaningful life outside the womb."

[T]he definition of a "viable" fetus is one that is capable of surviving outside the womb, but why is this the point at which the State's interest becomes compelling? If, as *Roe* held, a State's interest in protecting prenatal life is compelling "after viability," why isn't that interest "equally compelling before viability"? *Roe* did not say, and no explanation is apparent.

This arbitrary line has not found much support among philosophers and ethicists who have attempted to justify a right to abortion. Some have argued that a fetus should not be entitled to legal protection until it acquires the characteristics that they regard as defining what it means to be a "person." Among the characteristics that have been offered as essential attributes of "personhood" are sentience, self-awareness, the ability to reason, or some combination thereof. By this logic, it would be an open question whether even born individuals, including young children or those afflicted with certain developmental or medical conditions, merit protection as "persons." But even if one takes the view that "personhood" begins when a certain attribute or combination of attributes is acquired, it is very hard to see why viability should mark the point where "personhood" begins.

The most obvious problem with any such argument is that viability is heavily dependent on factors that have nothing to do with the characteristics of a fetus. One is the state of neonatal care at a particular point in time. Due to the development of new equipment and improved practices, the viability line has changed over the years. In the 19th century, a fetus may not have been viable until the 32d or 33d week of pregnancy or even later. When *Roe* was decided, viability was gauged at roughly 28 weeks. See 410 U. S., at 160. Today, respondents draw the line at 23 or 24 weeks. So, according to *Roe*'s logic, States now have a compelling interest in protecting a fetus with a gestational age of, say, 26 weeks, but in 1973 States did not have an interest in protecting an identical fetus. How can that be?

Viability also depends on the "quality of the available medical facilities." Thus, a 24-week-old fetus may be viable if a woman gives birth in a city with hospitals that provide advanced care for very premature babies, but if the woman travels to a remote area far from any such hospital, the fetus may no longer be viable. On what ground could the constitutional status of a fetus depend on the pregnant woman's location? And if viability is meant to mark a line having universal moral significance, can it be that a fetus that is viable in a big city in the United States has a privileged moral status not enjoyed by an identical fetus in a remote area of a poor country?

In addition, as the Court once explained, viability is not really a hard-and-fast line. A physician determining a particular fetus's odds of surviving outside the womb must consider "a number of variables," including "gestational age," "fetal weight," a woman's "general health and nutrition," the "quality of the available medical facilities," and other factors. It is thus "only with difficulty" that a physician can estimate the "probability" of a particular fetus's survival. And even if each fetus's probability of survival could be ascertained with certainty, settling on a "probabilit[y] of survival" that should count as "viability" is another matter. Is a fetus viable with a 10 percent chance of survival? 25 percent? 50 percent? Can such a judgment be made by a State? And can a State specify a gestational age limit that applies in all cases? Or must these difficult questions be left entirely to the individual "attending physician on the particular facts of the case before him"?

The viability line, which *Casey* termed *Roe*'s central rule, makes no sense, and it is telling that other countries almost uniformly eschew such a line. The Court thus asserted raw judicial power to impose, as a matter of constitutional law, a uniform viability rule that allowed the States less freedom to regulate abortion than the majority of western democracies enjoy. . . .

When *Casey* revisited *Roe* almost 20 years later, very little of *Roe*'s reasoning was defended or preserved. The Court abandoned any reliance on a privacy right and instead grounded the abortion right entirely on the Fourteenth Amendment's Due Process Clause. . . .The Court also made no real effort to remedy one of the greatest weaknesses in *Roe*'s analysis: its much-criticized discussion of viability. The Court retained what it called *Roe*'s "central holding"—that a State may not regulate pre-viability abortions for the purpose of protecting fetal life—but it provided no principled defense of the viability line. Instead, it merely rephrased what *Roe* had said, stating that viability marked the point at which "the independent existence of a second life can in reason and fairness be the object of state protection that now overrides the rights of the woman." Why "reason and fairness" demanded that the line be drawn at viability the Court did not explain. And the Justices who authored the controlling opinion conspicuously failed to say that they agreed with the viability rule; instead, they candidly acknowledged "the reservations [some] of us may have in reaffirming [that] holding of *Roe*."

The controlling opinion criticized and rejected *Roe*'s trimester scheme, and substituted a new "undue burden" test, but the basis for this test was obscure. And as we will explain, the test is full of ambiguities and is difficult to apply.

Casey, in short, either refused to reaffirm or rejected important aspects of *Roe*'s analysis, failed to remedy glaring deficiencies in *Roe*'s reasoning, endorsed what it termed *Roe*'s central holding while suggesting that a majority might not have thought it was correct, provided no new support for the abortion right other than *Roe*'s status as precedent, and imposed a new and problematic test with no firm grounding in constitutional text, history, or precedent.

As discussed below, *Casey* also deployed a novel version of the doctrine of *stare decisis*. This new doctrine did not account for the profound wrongness of the decision in *Roe*, and placed great weight on an intangible form of reliance with little if any basis in prior case law. *Stare decisis* does not command the preservation of such a decision.

C

Workability. Our precedents counsel that another important consideration in deciding whether a precedent should be overruled is whether the rule it imposes is workable—that is, whether it can be understood and applied in a consistent and predictable manner. *Casey*'s "undue burden" test has scored poorly on the workability scale.

Problems begin with the very concept of an "undue burden." As Justice Scalia noted in his *Casey* partial dissent, determining whether a burden is "due" or "undue" is "inherently standardless.". . . The *Casey* plurality tried to put meaning into the "undue burden" test by setting out three subsidiary rules, but these rules created their own problems. The first rule is that "a provision of law is invalid, if its purpose or effect is to place a *substantial obstacle* in the path of a woman seeking an abortion before the fetus attains viability." But whether a particular obstacle qualifies as "substantial" is often open to reasonable debate. In the sense relevant here, "substantial" means "of ample or considerable amount, quantity, or size." Random House Webster's Unabridged Dictionary 1897 (2d ed. 2001). Huge burdens are plainly "substantial," and trivial ones are not, but in between these extremes, there is a wide gray area.

[T]he second rule, which applies at all stages of a pregnancy, muddies things further. It states that measures designed "to ensure that the woman's choice is informed" are constitutional so long as they do not impose "an undue burden on the right." To the extent that this rule applies to pre-viability abortions, it overlaps with the first rule and appears to impose a different standard. Consider a law that imposes an insubstantial obstacle but serves little purpose. As applied to a pre-viability abortion, would such a regulation be constitutional on the ground that it does not impose a "*substantial* obstacle"? Or would it be unconstitutional on the ground that it creates an "*undue* burden" because the burden it imposes, though slight, outweighs its negligible benefits? *Casey* does not say, and this ambiguity would lead to confusion down the line. Compare *June Medical*, 591 U. S., at ___-___ (plurality opinion), with *id.*, at ___-___ (ROBERTS, C.J., concurring).

The third rule complicates the picture even more. Under that rule, "*[u]nnecessary health* regulations that have the purpose or effect of presenting a *substantial obstacle* to a woman seeking an abortion impose an *undue burden* on the right." . . . The term "necessary" has a range of meanings — from "essential" to merely "useful." See Black's Law Dictionary 928 (5th ed. 1979); American Heritage Dictionary of the English Language 877 (1971). *Casey* did not explain the sense in which the term is used in this rule.

[A]ll three rules . . . call on courts to examine a law's effect on women, but a regulation may have a very different impact on different women for a variety of reasons, including their places of residence, financial resources, family situations, work and personal obligations, knowledge about fetal development and abortion, psychological and emotional disposition and condition, and the firmness of their desire to obtain abortions. In order to determine whether a regulation presents a substantial obstacle to women, a court needs to know which set of women it should have in mind and how many of the women in this set must find that an obstacle is "substantial."

Casey provided no clear answer to these questions. It said that a regulation is unconstitutional if it imposes a substantial obstacle "in a large fraction of cases in which [it] is relevant," but there is obviously no clear line between a fraction that is "large" and one that is not. Nor is it clear what the Court meant by "cases in which" a regulation is "relevant." These ambiguities have caused confusion and disagreement.

The difficulty of applying *Casey*'s new rules surfaced in that very case. The controlling opinion found that Pennsylvania's 24-hour waiting period requirement and its informed-consent provision did not impose "undue burden[s]," but Justice Stevens, applying the same test, reached the opposite result. . . . The ambiguity of the "undue burden" test also produced disagreement in later cases. In *Whole Woman's Health*, the Court adopted the cost-benefit interpretation of the test, stating that "[t]he rule announced in *Casey* . . . requires that courts consider the burdens a law imposes on abortion access *together with the benefits those laws confer.*" But five years later, a majority of the Justices rejected that interpretation. See *June Medical.* Four Justices reaffirmed *Whole Woman's Health*'s instruction to "weigh" a law's "benefits" against "the burdens it imposes on abortion access." But THE CHIEF JUSTICE—who cast the deciding vote—argued that "[n]othing about *Casey* suggested that a weighing of costs and benefits of an abortion regulation was a job for the courts." And the four Justices in dissent rejected the plurality's interpretation of *Casey.* . . .

The experience of the Courts of Appeals provides further evidence that *Casey*'s "line between" permissible and unconstitutional restrictions "has proved to be impossible to draw with precision." . . . The Courts of Appeals have experienced particular difficulty in applying the large-fraction-of-relevant-cases test. They have criticized the assignment while reaching unpredictable results. And they have candidly outlined *Casey*'s many other problems.

Casey's "undue burden" test has proved to be unworkable. . . . Continued adherence to that standard would undermine, not advance, the "evenhanded, predictable, and consistent development of legal principles."

D

Effect on other areas of law. Roe and *Casey* have led to the distortion of many important but unrelated legal doctrines, and that effect provides further support for overruling those decisions. Members of this Court have repeatedly lamented that "no legal rule or doctrine is safe from ad hoc nullification by this Court when an occasion for its application arises in a case involving state regulation of abortion."

The Court's abortion cases have diluted the strict standard for facial constitutional challenges. They have ignored the Court's third-party standing doctrine. They have disregarded standard *res judicata* principles. They have flouted the ordinary rules on the severability of unconstitutional provisions, as well as the rule that statutes should be read where possible to avoid unconstitutionality. And they have distorted First Amendment doctrines. When vindicating a doctrinal innovation requires courts to engineer exceptions to longstanding background rules, the doctrine "has failed to deliver the 'principled and intelligible' development of the law that *stare decisis* purports to secure."

E

Reliance interests. We last consider whether overruling *Roe* and *Casey* will upend substantial reliance interests. Traditional reliance interests arise "where advance planning of great precision is most obviously a necessity." In *Casey*, the controlling opinion conceded that those traditional reliance interests were not implicated because getting an abortion is generally "unplanned activity," and "reproductive planning could take virtually immediate account of any sudden restoration of state authority to ban abortions." [W]e agree with the *Casey* plurality that conventional, concrete reliance interests are not present here.

Unable to find reliance in the conventional sense, the controlling opinion in *Casey* perceived a more intangible form of reliance. It wrote that "people [had] organized intimate relationships and made choices that define their views of themselves and their places in society . . . in reliance on the availability of abortion in the event that contraception should fail" and that "[t]he ability of women to participate equally in the economic and social life of the Nation has been facilitated by their ability to control their reproductive lives." But this Court is ill-equipped to assess "generalized assertions about the national psyche." *Casey*'s notion of reliance thus finds little support in our cases, which instead emphasize very concrete reliance interests, like those that develop in "cases involving property and contract rights."

When a concrete reliance interest is asserted, courts are equipped to evaluate the claim, but assessing the novel and intangible form of reliance endorsed by the *Casey* plurality is another matter. That form of reliance depends on an empirical question that is hard for anyone — and in particular, for a court — to assess, namely, the effect of the abortion right on society and in particular on the lives of women. The contending sides in this case make impassioned and conflicting arguments about the effects of the abortion right on the lives of women. The contending sides also make conflicting arguments about the status of the fetus. This Court has neither the authority nor the expertise to adjudicate those disputes, and the *Casey* plurality's speculations and weighing of the relative importance of the fetus and mother represent a departure from the "original constitutional proposition" that "courts do not substitute their social and economic beliefs for the judgment of legislative bodies." *Ferguson v. Skrupa*, 372 U.S. 726, 729-730 (1963). . . .

Women are not without electoral or political power. It is noteworthy that the percentage of women who register to vote and cast ballots is consistently higher than the percentage of men who do so. In the last election in November 2020, women, who make up around 51.5 percent of the population of Mississippi, constituted 55.5 percent of the voters who cast ballots.

Unable to show concrete reliance on *Roe* and *Casey* themselves, the Solicitor General suggests that overruling those decisions would "threaten the Court's precedents holding that the Due Process Clause protects other rights." . . . (citing *Obergefell*, *Lawrence*, [and] *Griswold*). . . . As even the *Casey* plurality recognized, "[a]bortion is a unique act" because it terminates "life or potential life." . . . And to ensure that our decision is not misunderstood or mischaracterized, we emphasize that our decision concerns the constitutional right to abortion and no other right. Nothing in this opinion should be understood to cast doubt on precedents that do not concern abortion.

IV

Having shown that traditional *stare decisis* factors do not weigh in favor of retaining *Roe* or *Casey*, we must address one final argument that featured prominently in the *Casey* plurality opinion.

The argument was cast in different terms, but stated simply, it was essentially as follows. The American people's belief in the rule of law would be shaken if they lost respect for this Court as an institution that decides important cases based on principle, not "social and political pressures." There is a special danger that the public will perceive a decision as having been made for unprincipled reasons when the Court overrules a controversial "watershed" decision, such as *Roe*. A decision overruling *Roe* would be perceived as having been made "under fire" and as a "surrender to political pressure," and therefore the preservation of public approval of the Court weighs heavily in favor of retaining *Roe*.

[T]he *Casey* plurality was certainly right that it is important for the public to perceive that our decisions are based on principle, and we should make every effort to achieve that objective by issuing opinions that carefully show how a proper understanding of the law leads to the results we reach. But we cannot exceed the scope of our authority under the Constitution, and we cannot allow our decisions to be affected by any extraneous influences such as concern about the public's reaction to our work. That is true both when we initially decide a constitutional issue *and* when we consider whether to overrule a prior decision. As Chief Justice Rehnquist explained, "The Judicial Branch derives its legitimacy, not from following public opinion, but from deciding by its best lights whether legislative enactments of the popular branches of Government comport with the Constitution. The doctrine of *stare decisis* is an adjunct of this duty, and should be no more subject to the vagaries of public opinion than is the basic judicial task.". . .

The *Casey* plurality "call[ed] the contending sides of a national controversy to end their national division," and claimed the authority to impose a permanent settlement of the issue of a constitutional abortion right simply by saying that the matter was closed. That unprecedented claim exceeded the power vested in us by the Constitution. . . . A precedent of this Court is subject to the usual principles of *stare decisis* under which adherence to precedent is the norm but not an inexorable command. If the rule were otherwise, erroneous decisions like *Plessy* and *Lochner* would still be the law. That is not how *stare decisis* operates.

The *Casey* plurality also misjudged the practical limits of this Court's influence. *Roe* certainly did not succeed in ending division on the issue of abortion. On the contrary, *Roe* "inflamed" a national issue that has remained bitterly divisive for the past half century. *Casey*, 505 U. S., at 995 (opinion of Scalia, J.); see also R. Ginsburg, Speaking in a Judicial Voice, 67 N. Y. U. L. Rev. 1185, 1208 (1992) (*Roe* may have "halted a political process," "prolonged divisiveness," and "deferred stable settlement of the issue"). And for the past 30 years, *Casey* has done the same.

Neither decision has ended debate over the issue of a constitutional right to obtain an abortion. Indeed, in this case, 26 States expressly ask us to overrule *Roe* and *Casey* and to return the issue of abortion to the people and their elected representatives. This Court's inability to end debate on the issue should not have been surprising. This Court cannot bring about the permanent resolution of a rancorous national controversy simply by dictating a settlement and telling the people to move on. Whatever influence the Court may have on public attitudes must stem from the strength of our opinions, not an attempt to exercise "raw judicial power." *Roe*, 410 U. S., at 222 (White, J., dissenting).

We do not pretend to know how our political system or society will respond to today's decision overruling *Roe* and *Casey*. And even if we could foresee what will happen, we would have no authority to let that knowledge influence our decision. We can only do our job, which is to interpret the law, apply longstanding principles of *stare decisis*, and decide this case accordingly.

We therefore hold that the Constitution does not confer a right to abortion. *Roe* and *Casey* must be overruled, and the authority to regulate abortion must be returned to the people and their elected representatives.

V

A

The dissent argues . . . . that the Court should never (or perhaps almost never) overrule an egregiously wrong constitutional precedent unless the Court can "poin[t] to major legal or factual changes undermining [the] decision's original basis." . . . [T]he dissent claims that *Brown v. Board of Education*, and other landmark cases overruling prior precedents "responded to changed law and to changed facts and attitudes that had taken hold throughout society." The unmistakable implication of this argument is that only the passage of time and new developments justified those decisions. Recognition that the cases they overruled were egregiously wrong on the day they were handed down was not enough.

The Court has never adopted this strange new version of *stare decisis* — and with good reason. Does the dissent really maintain that overruling *Plessy* was not justified until the country had experienced more than a half-century of state-sanctioned segregation and generations of Black school children had suffered all its effects?

Here is another example. On the dissent's view, it must have been wrong for *West Virginia Bd. of Ed. v. Barnette*, 319 U.S. 624, to overrule *Minersville School Dist. v. Gobitis*, 310 U.S. 586, a bare three years after it was handed down. In both cases, children who were Jehovah's Witnesses refused on religious grounds to salute the flag or recite the pledge of allegiance. The *Barnette* Court did not claim that its reexamination of the issue was prompted by any intervening legal or factual developments, so if the Court had followed the dissent's new version of *stare decisis,* it would have been compelled to adhere to *Gobitis* and countenance continued First Amendment violations for some unspecified period.

Precedents should be respected, but sometimes the Court errs, and occasionally the Court issues an important decision that is egregiously wrong. When that happens, *stare decisis* is not a straitjacket. And indeed, the dissent eventually admits that a decision *could* "be overruled just because it is terribly wrong," though the dissent does not explain when that would be so. . . .

B

[The Chief Justice, concurring in the judgment] would "leave for another day whether to reject any right to an abortion at all," and would hold only that if the Constitution protects any such right, the right ends once women have had "a reasonable opportunity" to obtain an abortion. The concurrence does not specify what period of time is sufficient to provide such an opportunity, but it would hold that 15 weeks, the period allowed under Mississippi's law, is enough — at least "absent rare circumstances."

There are serious problems with this approach, and it is revealing that nothing like it was recommended by either party. [B]oth parties and the Solicitor General have urged us either to reaffirm or overrule *Roe* and *Casey*. And when the specific approach advanced by the concurrence was broached at oral argument, both respondents and the Solicitor General emphatically rejected it. . . . The concurrence would do exactly what it criticizes *Roe* for doing: pulling "out of thin air" a test that "[n]o party or *amicus* asked the Court to adopt."

The concurrence's most fundamental defect is its failure to offer any principled basis for its approach. . . . [The viability] rule was a critical component of the holdings in *Roe* and *Casey*, and *stare decisis* is "a doctrine of preservation, not transformation," *Citizens United v. Federal Election Comm'n*, 558 U.S. 310, 384 (2010) (ROBERTS, C. J., concurring). Therefore, a new rule that discards the viability rule cannot be defended on *stare decisis* grounds.

If [the Chief Justice's proposed] rule is to become the law of the land, it must stand on its own, but the concurrence makes no attempt to show that this rule represents a correct interpretation of the Constitution. The concurrence does not claim that the right to a reasonable opportunity to obtain an abortion is " 'deeply rooted in this Nation's history and tradition' " and " 'implicit in the concept of ordered liberty.' " *Glucksberg*. Nor does it propound any other theory that could show that the Constitution supports its new rule. And if the Constitution protects a woman's right to obtain an abortion, the opinion does not explain why that right should end after the point at which all "reasonable" women will have decided whether to seek an abortion. While the concurrence is moved by a desire for judicial minimalism, "we cannot embrace a narrow ground of decision simply because it is narrow; it must also be right." *Citizens United*, 558 U. S., at 375 (ROBERTS, C. J., concurring). . . .

[I]f we held only that Mississippi's 15-week rule is constitutional, we would soon be called upon to pass on the constitutionality of a panoply of laws with shorter deadlines or no deadline at all. The "measured course" charted by the concurrence would be fraught with turmoil until the Court answered the question that the concurrence seeks to defer.

[I]f the period required to give women a "reasonable" opportunity to obtain an abortion were pegged, as the concurrence seems to suggest, at the point when a certain percentage of women make that choice, we would have to identify the relevant percentage. It would also be necessary to explain what the concurrence means when it refers to "rare circumstances" that might justify an exception.

And if this new right aims to give women a reasonable opportunity to get an abortion, it would be necessary to decide whether factors other than promptness in deciding might have a bearing on whether such an opportunity was available.

In sum, the concurrence's quest for a middle way would only put off the day when we would be forced to confront the question we now decide. The turmoil wrought by *Roe* and *Casey* would be prolonged. It is far better—for this Court and the country—to face up to the real issue without further delay.

VI

[U]nder our precedents, rational-basis review is the appropriate standard for such challenges. . . . It follows that the States may regulate abortion for legitimate reasons, and when such regulations are challenged under the Constitution, courts cannot "substitute their social and economic beliefs for the judgment of legislative bodies." *Ferguson*; see also *Dandridge v. Williams*, 397 U.S. 471, 484-486 (1970); *United States v. Carolene Products Co.*, 304 U.S. 144, 152 (1938). . . .

A law regulating abortion, like other health and welfare laws, is entitled to a "strong presumption of validity." It must be sustained if there is a rational basis on which the legislature could have thought that it would serve legitimate state interests. These legitimate interests include respect for and preservation of prenatal life at all stages of development, the protection of maternal health and safety; the elimination of particularly gruesome or barbaric medical procedures; the preservation of the integrity of the medical profession; the mitigation of fetal pain; and the prevention of discrimination on the basis of race, sex, or disability.

These legitimate interests justify Mississippi's Gestational Age Act. . . . The legislature also found that abortions performed after 15 weeks typically use the dilation and evacuation procedure, and the legislature found the use of this procedure "for nontherapeutic or elective reasons [to be] a barbaric practice, dangerous for the maternal patient, and demeaning to the medical profession." These legitimate interests provide a rational basis for the Gestational Age Act, and it follows that respondents' constitutional challenge must fail.

VII

We end this opinion where we began. Abortion presents a profound moral question. The Constitution does not prohibit the citizens of each State from regulating or prohibiting abortion. *Roe* and *Casey* arrogated that authority. We now overrule those decisions and return that authority to the people and their elected representatives.

The judgment of the Fifth Circuit is reversed, and the case is remanded for further proceedings consistent with this opinion.

It is so ordered.

Justice THOMAS, concurring.

I join the opinion of the Court because it correctly holds that there is no constitutional right to abortion. . . . "[T]he idea that the Framers of the Fourteenth

Amendment understood the Due Process Clause to protect a right to abortion is farcical." *June Medical Services L. L.C. v. Russo*, 591 U.S. ___, ___ (2020) (THOMAS, J., dissenting).

I write separately to emphasize a second, more fundamental reason why there is no abortion guarantee lurking in the Due Process Clause. Considerable historical evidence indicates that "due process of law" merely required executive and judicial actors to comply with legislative enactments and the common law when depriving a person of life, liberty, or property. Other sources, by contrast, suggest that "due process of law" prohibited legislatures "from authorizing the deprivation of a person's life, liberty, or property without providing him the customary procedures to which freemen were entitled by the old law of England." Either way, the Due Process Clause at most guarantees *process*. It does not, as the Court's substantive due process cases suppose, "forbi[d] the government to infringe certain 'fundamental' liberty interests *at all*, no matter what process is provided."

As I have previously explained, "substantive due process" is an oxymoron that "lack[s] any basis in the Constitution." "The notion that a constitutional provision that guarantees only 'process' before a person is deprived of life, liberty, or property could define the substance of those rights strains credulity for even the most casual user of words." The resolution of this case is thus straightforward. Because the Due Process Clause does not secure *any* substantive rights, it does not secure a right to abortion.

The Court today declines to disturb substantive due process jurisprudence generally or the doctrine's application in other, specific contexts. . . . I agree that "[n]othing in [the Court's] opinion should be understood to cast doubt on precedents that do not concern abortion." For that reason, in future cases, we should reconsider all of this Court's substantive due process precedents, including *Griswold*, *Lawrence*, and *Obergefell*. Because any substantive due process decision is "demonstrably erroneous," we have a duty to "correct the error" established in those precedents. After overruling these demonstrably erroneous decisions, the question would remain whether other constitutional provisions guarantee the myriad rights that our substantive due process cases have generated. For example, we could consider whether any of the rights announced in this Court's substantive due process cases are "privileges or immunities of citizens of the United States" protected by the Fourteenth Amendment. To answer that question, we would need to decide important antecedent questions, including whether the Privileges or Immunities Clause protects *any* rights that are not enumerated in the Constitution and, if so, how to identify those rights. That said, even if the Clause does protect unenumerated rights, the Court conclusively demonstrates that abortion is not one of them under any plausible interpretive approach.

Moreover, apart from being a demonstrably incorrect reading of the Due Process Clause, the "legal fiction" of substantive due process is "particularly dangerous." At least three dangers favor jettisoning the doctrine entirely.

First, "substantive due process exalts judges at the expense of the People from whom they derive their authority.". . . The Court divines new rights in line with "its own, extraconstitutional value preferences" and nullifies state laws that do not align with the judicially created guarantees. . . .

Second, substantive due process distorts other areas of constitutional law. For example, once this Court identifies a "fundamental" right for one class of individuals, it invokes the Equal Protection Clause to demand exacting scrutiny of statutes that deny the right to others. See, *e.g.,Eisenstadt v. Baird*. Statutory classifications implicating certain "nonfundamental" rights, meanwhile, receive only cursory review. Similarly, this Court deems unconstitutionally "vague" or "overbroad" those laws that impinge on its preferred rights, while letting slide those laws that implicate supposedly lesser values. . . . Therefore, regardless of the doctrinal context, the Court often "demand[s] extra justifications for encroachments" on "preferred rights" while "relax[ing] purportedly higher standards of review for less preferred rights." Substantive due process is the core inspiration for many of the Court's constitutionally unmoored policy judgments.

Third, substantive due process is often wielded to "disastrous ends." For instance, in *Dred Scott v. Sandford*, 19 How. 393 (1857), the Court invoked a species of substantive due process to announce that Congress was powerless to emancipate slaves brought into the federal territories. While *Dred Scott* "was overruled on the battlefields of the Civil War and by constitutional amendment after Appomattox," that overruling was "[p]urchased at the price of immeasurable human suffering." Now today, the Court rightly overrules *Roe* and *Casey*—two of this Court's "most notoriously incorrect" substantive due process decisions—after more than 63 million abortions have been performed. The harm caused by this Court's forays into substantive due process remains immeasurable.

[I]n future cases, we should "follow the text of the Constitution, which sets forth certain substantive rights that cannot be taken away, and adds, beyond that, a right to due process when life, liberty, or property is to be taken away." Substantive due process conflicts with that textual command and has harmed our country in many ways. Accordingly, we should eliminate it from our jurisprudence at the earliest opportunity.

Justice KAVANAUGH, concurring.

I write separately to explain my additional views about why *Roe* was wrongly decided, why *Roe* should be overruled at this time, and the future implications of today's decision. . . .

I

Abortion is a profoundly difficult and contentious issue because it presents an irreconcilable conflict between the interests of a pregnant woman who seeks an abortion and the interests in protecting fetal life. The interests on both sides of the abortion issue are extraordinarily weighty. . . .

The issue before this Court, however, is not the policy or morality of abortion. The issue before this Court is what the Constitution says about abortion.

The Constitution does not take sides on the issue of abortion. . . . The text of the Constitution does not refer to or encompass abortion. To be sure, this Court has held that the Constitution protects unenumerated rights that are deeply rooted in this Nation's history and tradition, and implicit in the concept of ordered liberty. But a right to abortion is not deeply rooted in American history and tradition, as the Court today thoroughly explains. . . . The Court's opinion today also recounts the pre-constitutional common-law history in England. That English history supplies background information on the issue of abortion. As I see it, the dispositive point in analyzing American history and tradition for purposes of the Fourteenth Amendment inquiry is that abortion was largely prohibited in most American States as of 1868 when the Fourteenth Amendment was ratified, and that abortion remained largely prohibited in most American States until *Roe* was decided in 1973. [relocated footnote—eds.]

On the question of abortion, the Constitution is therefore neither pro-life nor pro-choice. The Constitution is neutral and leaves the issue for the people and their elected representatives to resolve through the democratic process in the States or Congress—like the numerous other difficult questions of American social and economic policy that the Constitution does not address.

Because the Constitution is neutral on the issue of abortion, this Court also must be scrupulously neutral. The nine unelected Members of this Court do not possess the constitutional authority to override the democratic process and to decree either a pro-life or a pro-choice abortion policy for all 330 million people in the United States.

Instead of adhering to the Constitution's neutrality, the Court in *Roe* took sides on the issue and unilaterally decreed that abortion was legal throughout the United States up to the point of viability (about 24 weeks of pregnancy). The Court's decision today properly returns the Court to a position of neutrality and restores the people's authority to address the issue of abortion through the processes of democratic self-government established by the Constitution.

Some *amicus* briefs argue that the Court today should not only overrule *Roe* and return to a position of judicial neutrality on abortion, but should go further and hold that the Constitution *outlaws* abortion throughout the United States. No Justice of this Court has ever advanced that position. I respect those who advocate for that position, just as I respect those who argue that this Court should hold that the Constitution legalizes pre-viability abortion throughout the United States. But both positions are wrong as a constitutional matter, in my view. The Constitution neither outlaws abortion nor legalizes abortion.

To be clear, then, the Court's decision today *does not outlaw* abortion throughout the United States. On the contrary, the Court's decision properly leaves the question of abortion for the people and their elected representatives in the democratic process. . . .

After today's decision, all of the States may evaluate the competing interests and decide how to address this consequential issue. . . . In his dissent in *Roe*, Justice Rehnquist indicated that an exception to a State's restriction on abortion would be constitutionally required when an abortion is necessary to save the life of the mother. See *Roe v. Wade*, 410 U.S. 113, 173 (1973). Abortion statutes traditionally and currently provide for an exception when an abortion is necessary to protect the life of the mother. Some statutes also provide other exceptions. [relocated footnote — eds.]

In arguing for a *constitutional* right to abortion that would override the people's choices in the democratic process, the plaintiff Jackson Women's Health Organization and its *amici* emphasize that the Constitution does not freeze the American people's rights as of 1791 or 1868. I fully agree. To begin, I agree that constitutional rights apply to situations that were unforeseen in 1791 or 1868 — such as applying the First Amendment to the Internet or the Fourth Amendment to cars. . . . . [But] [t]he Constitution does not grant the nine unelected Members of this Court the unilateral authority to rewrite the Constitution to create new rights and liberties based on our own moral or policy views. . . . This Court therefore does not possess the authority either to declare a constitutional right to abortion *or* to declare a constitutional prohibition of abortion. . . . In my respectful view, the Court in *Roe* therefore erred by taking sides on the issue of abortion.

II

The more difficult question in this case is *stare decisis* — that is, whether to overrule the *Roe* decision. . . .

When precisely should the Court overrule an erroneous constitutional precedent? The history of *stare decisis* in this Court establishes that a constitutional precedent may be overruled only when (i) the prior decision is not just wrong, but is egregiously wrong, (ii) the prior decision has caused significant negative jurisprudential or real-world consequences, and (iii) overruling the prior decision would not unduly upset legitimate reliance interests.

Applying those factors, I agree with the Court today that *Roe* should be overruled. The Court in *Roe* erroneously assigned itself the authority to decide a critically important moral and policy issue that the Constitution does not grant this Court the authority to decide. As Justice Byron White succinctly explained, *Roe* was "an improvident and extravagant exercise of the power of judicial review" because "nothing in the language or history of the Constitution" supports a constitutional right to abortion. *Bolton*, 410 U. S., at 221–222 (dissenting opinion).

Of course, the fact that a precedent is wrong, even egregiously wrong, does not alone mean that the precedent should be overruled. But as the Court today explains, *Roe* has caused significant negative jurisprudential and real-world consequences. By taking sides on a difficult and contentious issue on which the Constitution is neutral, *Roe* overreached and exceeded this Court's constitutional authority; gravely distorted the Nation's understanding of this Court's proper constitutional role; and caused significant harm to what *Roe* itself recognized as the State's "important and legitimate interest" in protecting fetal life. All of that explains why tens of millions of Americans — and the 26 States that explicitly ask the Court to overrule *Roe* — do not accept *Roe* even 49 years later. Under the Court's longstanding *stare decisis* principles, *Roe* should be overruled.

I also agree with the Court's conclusion today with respect to reliance. Broad notions of societal reliance have been invoked in support of *Roe*, but the Court has not analyzed reliance in that way in the past. For example, American businesses and workers relied on *Lochner v. New York*, 198 U.S. 45 (1905), and *Adkins v. Children's Hospital of D. C.*, 261 U.S. 525 (1923), to construct a laissez-faire economy that was free of substantial regulation. In *West Coast Hotel Co. v. Parrish*, 300 U.S. 379 (1937), the Court nonetheless overruled *Adkins* and in effect *Lochner*. An entire region of the country relied on *Plessy v. Ferguson*, 163 U.S. 537 (1896), to enforce a system of racial segregation. In *Brown v. Board of Education*, 347 U.S. 483 (1954), the Court overruled *Plessy*. Much of American society was built around the traditional view of marriage that was upheld in *Baker v. Nelson*, 409 U.S. 810 (1972), and that was reflected in laws ranging from tax laws to estate laws to family laws. In *Obergefell v. Hodges*, 576 U.S. 644 (2015), the Court nonetheless overruled *Baker*. [relocated footnote—eds.]

But the *stare decisis* analysis here is somewhat more complicated because of *Casey*. . . . I have deep and unyielding respect for the Justices who wrote the *Casey* plurality opinion. And I respect the *Casey* plurality's good-faith effort to locate some middle ground or compromise that could resolve this controversy for America.

But as has become increasingly evident over time, *Casey*'s well-intentioned effort did not resolve the abortion debate. The national division has not ended. In recent years, a significant number of States have enacted abortion restrictions that directly conflict with *Roe*. Those laws cannot be dismissed as political stunts or as outlier laws. Those numerous state laws collectively represent the sincere and deeply held views of tens of millions of Americans who continue to fervently believe that allowing abortions up to 24 weeks is far too radical and far too extreme, and does not sufficiently account for what *Roe* itself recognized as the State's "important and legitimate interest" in protecting fetal life. In this case, moreover, a majority of the States—26 in all—ask the Court to overrule *Roe* and return the abortion issue to the States.

In short, *Casey*'s *stare decisis* analysis rested in part on a predictive judgment about the future development of state laws and of the people's views on the abortion issue. But that predictive judgment has not borne out. As the Court today explains, the experience over the last 30 years conflicts with *Casey*'s predictive judgment and therefore undermines *Casey*'s precedential force.

To be clear, public opposition to a prior decision is not a basis for overruling (or reaffirming) that decision. Rather, the question of whether to overrule a precedent must be analyzed under this Court's traditional *stare decisis* factors. The only point here is that *Casey* adopted a special *stare decisis* principle with respect to *Roe* based on the idea of resolving the national controversy and ending the national division over abortion. The continued and significant opposition to *Roe*, as reflected in the laws and positions of numerous States, is relevant to assessing *Casey* on its own terms. [relocated footnote—eds.]

In any event, although *Casey* is relevant to the *stare decisis* analysis, the question of whether to overrule *Roe* cannot be dictated by *Casey* alone. To illustrate that *stare decisis* point, consider an example. Suppose that in 1924 this Court had expressly reaffirmed *Plessy v. Ferguson* and upheld the States' authority to segregate people on the basis of race. Would the Court in *Brown* some 30 years later in 1954 have reaffirmed *Plessy* and upheld racially segregated schools simply because of that intervening 1924 precedent? Surely the answer is no. . . .

III

[T]he parties' arguments have raised other related questions, and I address some of them here.

First is the question of how this decision will affect other precedents involving issues such as contraception and marriage. . . . I emphasize what the Court today states: Overruling *Roe* does *not* mean the overruling of [*Griswold*, *Eisenstadt*, and *Loving*], and does *not* threaten or cast doubt on those precedents.

Second, as I see it, some of the other abortion-related legal questions raised by today's decision are not especially difficult as a constitutional matter. For example, may a State bar a resident of that State from traveling to another State to obtain an abortion? In my view, the answer is no based on the constitutional right to interstate travel. May a State retroactively impose liability or punishment for an abortion that occurred before today's decision takes effect? In my view, the answer is no based on the Due Process Clause or the *Ex Post Facto* Clause. Cf. *Bouie v. City of Columbia*, 378 U.S. 347 (1964). . . .

To be sure, many Americans will disagree with the Court's decision today. That would be true no matter how the Court decided this case. Both sides on the abortion issue believe sincerely and passionately in the rightness of their cause. Especially in those difficult and fraught circumstances, the Court must scrupulously adhere to the Constitution's neutral position on the issue of abortion. . . . [T]he Constitution is neither pro-life nor pro-choice. The Constitution is neutral, and this Court likewise must be scrupulously neutral. The Court today properly heeds the constitutional principle of judicial neutrality and returns the issue of abortion to the people and their elected representatives in the democratic process.

Chief Justice ROBERTS, concurring in the judgment.

. . . I would take a more measured course. I agree with the Court that the viability line established by *Roe* and *Casey* should be discarded under a straightforward *stare decisis* analysis. That line never made any sense. Our abortion precedents describe the right at issue as a woman's right to choose to terminate her pregnancy. That right should therefore extend far enough to ensure a reasonable opportunity to choose, but need not extend any further—certainly not all the way to viability. Mississippi's law allows a woman three months to obtain an abortion, well beyond the point at which it is considered "late" to discover a pregnancy. . . . I see no sound basis for questioning the adequacy of that opportunity.

But that is all I would say, out of adherence to a simple yet fundamental principle of judicial restraint: If it is not necessary to decide more to dispose of a case, then it is necessary *not* to decide more. Perhaps we are not always perfect in following that command, and certainly there are cases that warrant an exception. But this is not one of them. Surely we should adhere closely to principles of judicial restraint here, where the broader path the Court chooses entails repudiating a constitutional right we have not only previously recognized, but also expressly reaffirmed applying the doctrine of *stare decisis*. . . .

I

[T]his Court seriously erred in *Roe* in adopting viability as the earliest point at which a State may legislate to advance its substantial interests in the area of abortion. *Roe* set forth a rigid three-part framework anchored to viability, which more closely resembled a regulatory code than a body of constitutional law. That framework, moreover, came out of thin air. . . . It is thus hardly surprising that neither *Roe* nor *Casey* made a persuasive or even colorable argument for why the time for terminating a pregnancy must extend to viability. The Court's jurisprudence on this issue is a textbook illustration of the perils of deciding a question neither presented nor briefed. As has been often noted, *Roe*'s defense of the line boiled down to the circular assertion that the State's interest is compelling only when an unborn child can live outside the womb, because that is when the unborn child can live outside the womb. . . .

Twenty years later, the best defense of the viability line the *Casey* plurality could conjure up was workability. Although the plurality attempted to add more content by opining that "it might be said that a woman who fails to act before viability has consented to the State's intervention on behalf of the developing child," that mere suggestion provides no basis for choosing viability as the critical tipping point. A similar implied consent argument could be made with respect to a law banning abortions after fifteen weeks, well beyond the point at which nearly all women are aware that they are pregnant. The dissent, which would retain the viability line, offers no justification for it either.

This Court's jurisprudence since *Casey,* moreover, has "eroded" the "underpinnings" of the viability line, such as they were. The viability line is a relic of a time when we recognized only two state interests warranting regulation of abortion: maternal health and protection of "potential life." That changed with *Gonzales v. Carhart*, 550 U.S. 124 (2007). There, we recognized a broader array of interests, such as drawing "a bright line that clearly distinguishes abortion and infanticide," maintaining societal ethics, and preserving the integrity of the medical profession. The viability line has nothing to do with advancing such permissible goals. . . .

Consider, for example, statutes passed in a number of jurisdictions that forbid abortions after twenty weeks of pregnancy, premised on the theory that a fetus can feel pain at that stage of development. . . . Assuming that prevention of fetal pain is a legitimate state interest after *Gonzales*, there seems to be no reason why viability would be relevant to the permissibility of such laws. The same is true of laws designed to "protect[] the integrity and ethics of the medical profession" and restrict procedures likely to "coarsen society" to the "dignity of human life." Mississippi's law, for instance, was premised in part on the legislature's finding that the "dilation and evacuation" procedure is a "barbaric practice, dangerous for the maternal patient, and demeaning to the medical profession." That procedure accounts for most abortions performed after the first trimester — two weeks before the period at issue in this case — and "involve[s] the use of surgical instruments to crush and tear the unborn child apart." Again, it would make little sense to focus on viability when evaluating a law based on these permissible goals.

In short, the viability rule was created outside the ordinary course of litigation, is and always has been completely unreasoned, and fails to take account of state interests since recognized as legitimate. It is indeed "telling that other countries almost uniformly eschew" a viability line. Only a handful of countries, among them China and North Korea, permit elective abortions after twenty weeks; the rest have coalesced around a 12-week line. See The World's Abortion Laws, Center for Reproductive Rights (Feb. 23, 2021) (online source archived at www .supremecourt.gov) (Canada, China, Iceland, Guinea-Bissau, the Netherlands, North Korea, Singapore, and Vietnam permit elective abortions after twenty weeks). The Court rightly rejects the arbitrary viability rule today.

II

None of this, however, requires that we also take the dramatic step of altogether eliminating the abortion right first recognized in *Roe*. Mississippi itself previously argued as much to this Court in this litigation. . . .[I]t went out of its way to make clear that it was *not* asking the Court to repudiate entirely the right to choose whether to terminate a pregnancy: "To be clear, the questions presented in this petition do not require the Court to overturn *Roe* or *Casey*.". . . After we granted certiorari, however, Mississippi changed course. . . . The Court now rewards that gambit, noting three times that the parties presented "no half-measures" and argued that "we must either reaffirm or overrule *Roe* and *Casey*." Given those two options, the majority picks the latter. . . .

Our established practice is instead not to "formulate a rule of constitutional law broader than is required by the precise facts to which it is to be applied." . . . Following that "fundamental principle of judicial restraint," we should begin with the narrowest basis for disposition, proceeding to consider a broader one only if necessary to resolve the case at hand. . . . Here, there is a clear path to deciding this case correctly without overruling *Roe* all the way down to the studs: recognize that the viability line must be discarded, as the majority rightly does, and leave for another day whether to reject any right to an abortion at all. . . . .

Of course, such an approach would not be available if the rationale of *Roe* and *Casey* was inextricably entangled with and dependent upon the viability standard. It is not. Our precedents in this area ground the abortion right in a woman's "right to choose.". . . . If that is the basis for *Roe*, *Roe*'s viability line should be scrutinized from the same perspective. And there is nothing inherent in the right to choose that requires it to extend to viability or any other point, so long as a real choice is provided. . . . To be sure, in reaffirming the right to an abortion, *Casey* termed the viability rule *Roe*'s "central holding." Other cases of ours have repeated that language. But simply declaring it does not make it so. The question in *Roe* was whether there was any right to abortion in the Constitution. How far the right extended was a concern that was separate and subsidiary, and — not surprisingly — entirely unbriefed. . . .The viability line is a separate rule fleshing out the metes and bounds of *Roe*'s core holding. Applying principles of *stare decisis*, I would excise that additional rule — and only that rule — from our jurisprudence. . . .

Overruling the subsidiary rule is sufficient to resolve this case in Mississippi's favor. The law at issue allows abortions up through fifteen weeks, providing an adequate opportunity to exercise the right *Roe* protects. By the time a pregnant woman has reached that point, her pregnancy is well into the second trimester. Pregnancy tests are now inexpensive and accurate, and a woman ordinarily discovers she is pregnant by six weeks of gestation. Almost all know by the end of the first trimester. Safe and effective abortifacients, moreover, are now readily available, particularly during those early stages. Given all this, it is no surprise that the vast majority of abortions happen in the first trimester. Presumably most of the remainder would also take place earlier if later abortions were not a legal option. Ample evidence thus suggests that a 15-week ban provides sufficient time, absent rare circumstances, for a woman "to decide for herself" whether to terminate her pregnancy.

III

[T]he Court's decision to overrule *Roe* and *Casey* is a serious jolt to the legal system — regardless of how you view those cases. A narrower decision rejecting the misguided viability line would be markedly less unsettling, and nothing more is needed to decide this case.

Our cases say that the effect of overruling a precedent on reliance interests is a factor to consider in deciding whether to take such a step, and respondents argue that generations of women have relied on the right to an abortion in organizing their relationships and planning their futures. The Court questions whether these concerns are pertinent under our precedents, but the issue would not even arise with a decision rejecting only the viability line: It cannot reasonably be argued that women have shaped their lives in part on the assumption that they would be able to abort up to viability, as opposed to fifteen weeks.

In support of its holding, the Court cites three seminal constitutional decisions that involved overruling prior precedents: *Brown v. Board of Education*, 347 U.S. 483 (1954), *West Virginia Bd. of Ed. v. Barnette*, 319 U.S. 624 (1943), and *West Coast Hotel Co. v. Parrish*, 300 U.S. 379 (1937). See *ante*, at 40-41. The opinion in *Brown* was unanimous and eleven pages long; this one is neither. *Barnette* was decided only three years after the decision it overruled, three

Justices having had second thoughts. And *West Coast Hotel* was issued against a backdrop of unprecedented economic despair that focused attention on the fundamental flaws of existing precedent. It also was part of a sea change in this Court's interpretation of the Constitution, "signal[ing] the demise of an entire line of important precedents,"—a feature the Court expressly disclaims in today's decision, None of these leading cases, in short, provides a template for what the Court does today.

The Court says we should consider whether to overrule *Roe* and *Casey* now, because if we delay we would be forced to consider the issue again in short order. There would be "turmoil" until we did so, according to the Court, because of existing state laws with "shorter deadlines or no deadline at all." But under the narrower approach proposed here, state laws outlawing abortion altogether would still violate binding precedent. And to the extent States have laws that set the cutoff date earlier than fifteen weeks, any litigation over that timeframe would proceed free of the distorting effect that the viability rule has had on our constitutional debate. The same could be true, for that matter, with respect to legislative consideration in the States. We would then be free to exercise our discretion in deciding whether and when to take up the issue, from a more informed perspective. . . .

Justice BREYER, Justice SOTOMAYOR, and Justice KAGAN, dissenting.

For half a century, *Roe v. Wade*, 410 U.S. 113 (1973), and *Planned Parenthood of Southeastern Pa. v. Casey*, 505 U.S. 833 (1992), have protected the liberty and equality of women. *Roe* held, and *Casey* reaffirmed, that the Constitution safeguards a woman's right to decide for herself whether to bear a child. *Roe* held, and *Casey* reaffirmed, that in the first stages of pregnancy, the government could not make that choice for women. The government could not control a woman's body or the course of a woman's life: It could not determine what the woman's future would be. Respecting a woman as an autonomous being, and granting her full equality, meant giving her substantial choice over this most personal and most consequential of all life decisions.

Roe and *Casey* well understood the difficulty and divisiveness of the abortion issue. . . . So the Court struck a balance, as it often does when values and goals compete. It held that the State could prohibit abortions after fetal viability, so long as the ban contained exceptions to safeguard a woman's life or health. It held that even before viability, the State could regulate the abortion procedure in multiple and meaningful ways. But until the viability line was crossed, the Court held, a State could not impose a "substantial obstacle" on a woman's "right to elect the procedure" as she (not the government) thought proper, in light of all the circumstances and complexities of her own life.

Today, the Court discards that balance. It says that from the very moment of fertilization, a woman has no rights to speak of. A State can force her to bring a pregnancy to term, even at the steepest personal and familial costs. An abortion restriction, the majority holds, is permissible whenever rational, the lowest level

of scrutiny known to the law. And because, as the Court has often stated, protecting fetal life is rational, States will feel free to enact all manner of restrictions.
The Mississippi law at issue here bars abortions after the 15th week of pregnancy. Under the majority's ruling, though, another State's law could do so after
ten weeks, or five or three or one — or, again, from the moment of fertilization.
States have already passed such laws, in anticipation of today's ruling. More
will follow. Some States have enacted laws extending to all forms of abortion
procedure, including taking medication in one's own home. They have passed
laws without any exceptions for when the woman is the victim of rape or incest.
Under those laws, a woman will have to bear her rapist's child or a young girl
her father's — no matter if doing so will destroy her life. So too, after today's ruling, some States may compel women to carry to term a fetus with severe physical anomalies — for example, one afflicted with Tay-Sachs disease, sure to die
within a few years of birth. States may even argue that a prohibition on abortion
need make no provision for protecting a woman from risk of death or physical
harm. Across a vast array of circumstances, a State will be able to impose its
moral choice on a woman and coerce her to give birth to a child.

Enforcement of all these draconian restrictions will also be left largely to
the States' devices. A State can of course impose criminal penalties on abortion providers, including lengthy prison sentences. But some States will not stop
there. Perhaps, in the wake of today's decision, a state law will criminalize the
woman's conduct too, incarcerating or fining her for daring to seek or obtain
an abortion. And as Texas has recently shown, a State can turn neighbor against
neighbor, enlisting fellow citizens in the effort to root out anyone who tries to get
an abortion, or to assist another in doing so.

The majority tries to hide the geographically expansive effects of its holding.
Today's decision, the majority says, permits "each State" to address abortion
as it pleases. That is cold comfort, of course, for the poor woman who cannot
get the money to fly to a distant State for a procedure. Above all others, women
lacking financial resources will suffer from today's decision. In any event, interstate restrictions will also soon be in the offing. After this decision, some States
may block women from traveling out of State to obtain abortions, or even from
receiving abortion medications from out of State. Some may criminalize efforts,
including the provision of information or funding, to help women gain access to
other States' abortion services. Most threatening of all, no language in today's
decision stops the Federal Government from prohibiting abortions nationwide,
once again from the moment of conception and without exceptions for rape or
incest. If that happens, "the views of [an individual State's] citizens" will not
matter. The challenge for a woman will be to finance a trip not to "New York [or]
California" but to Toronto.

Whatever the exact scope of the coming laws, one result of today's decision
is certain: the curtailment of women's rights, and of their status as free and equal
citizens. Yesterday, the Constitution guaranteed that a woman confronted with
an unplanned pregnancy could (within reasonable limits) make her own decision

about whether to bear a child, with all the life-transforming consequences that act involves. And in thus safeguarding each woman's reproductive freedom, the Constitution also protected "[t]he ability of women to participate equally in [this Nation's] economic and social life." *Casey*. But no longer. As of today, this Court holds, a State can always force a woman to give birth, prohibiting even the earliest abortions. A State can thus transform what, when freely undertaken, is a wonder into what, when forced, may be a nightmare. Some women, especially women of means, will find ways around the State's assertion of power. Others — those without money or childcare or the ability to take time off from work — will not be so fortunate. Maybe they will try an unsafe method of abortion, and come to physical harm, or even die. Maybe they will undergo pregnancy and have a child, but at significant personal or familial cost. At the least, they will incur the cost of losing control of their lives. The Constitution will, today's majority holds, provide no shield, despite its guarantees of liberty and equality for all.

And no one should be confident that this majority is done with its work. The right *Roe* and *Casey* recognized does not stand alone. To the contrary, the Court has linked it for decades to other settled freedoms involving bodily integrity, familial relationships, and procreation. Most obviously, the right to terminate a pregnancy arose straight out of the right to purchase and use contraception. See *Griswold*; *Eisenstadt*. In turn, those rights led, more recently, to rights of same-sex intimacy and marriage. See *Lawrence*; *Obergefell*. They are all part of the same constitutional fabric, protecting autonomous decisionmaking over the most personal of life decisions. The majority (or to be more accurate, most of it) is eager to tell us today that nothing it does "cast[s] doubt on precedents that do not concern abortion." *Ante*, at 66; cf. *ante*, at 3 (THOMAS, J., concurring) (advocating the overruling of *Griswold*, *Lawrence*, and *Obergefell*). But how could that be? The lone rationale for what the majority does today is that the right to elect an abortion is not "deeply rooted in history": Not until *Roe*, the majority argues, did people think abortion fell within the Constitution's guarantee of liberty. The same could be said, though, of most of the rights the majority claims it is not tampering with. The majority could write just as long an opinion showing, for example, that until the mid-20th century, "there was no support in American law for a constitutional right to obtain [contraceptives]." So one of two things must be true. Either the majority does not really believe in its own reasoning. Or if it does, all rights that have no history stretching back to the mid-19th century are insecure. Either the mass of the majority's opinion is hypocrisy, or additional constitutional rights are under threat. It is one or the other.

One piece of evidence on that score seems especially salient: The majority's cavalier approach to overturning this Court's precedents. *Stare decisis* is the Latin phrase for a foundation stone of the rule of law: that things decided should stay decided unless there is a very good reason for change. It is a doctrine of judicial modesty and humility. Those qualities are not evident in today's opinion. The majority has no good reason for the upheaval in law and society it sets off. *Roe* and *Casey* have been the law of the land for decades, shaping women's expectations of their choices when an unplanned pregnancy occurs. Women have relied on the availability of abortion both in structuring their relationships and in planning their lives. The legal framework *Roe* and *Casey* developed to balance the competing interests in this sphere has proved workable in courts across the country. No recent developments, in either law or fact, have eroded or cast doubt on those precedents. Nothing, in short, has changed. Indeed, the Court in *Casey* already found all of that to be true. *Casey* is a precedent about precedent. It reviewed the same arguments made here in support of overruling *Roe*, and it found that doing so was not warranted. The Court reverses course today for one reason and one reason only: because the composition of this Court has changed. *Stare decisis*, this Court has often said, "contributes to the actual and perceived integrity of the judicial process" by ensuring that decisions are "founded in the law rather than in the proclivities of individuals." Today, the proclivities of individuals rule. The Court departs from its obligation to faithfully and impartially apply the law. We dissent.

I

[T]o hear the majority tell the tale, *Roe* and *Casey* are aberrations: They came from nowhere, went nowhere—and so are easy to excise from this Nation's constitutional law. That is not true. . . . they are rooted in—and themselves led to—other rights giving individuals control over their bodies and their most personal and intimate associations. . . . *Roe* and *Casey* were from the beginning, and are even more now, embedded in core constitutional concepts of individual freedom, and of the equal rights of citizens to decide on the shape of their lives. Those legal concepts, one might even say, have gone far toward defining what it means to be an American. For in this Nation, we do not believe that a government controlling all private choices is compatible with a free people. . . .We believe in a Constitution that puts some issues off limits to majority rule. Even in the face of public opposition, we uphold the right of individuals—yes, including women—to make their own choices and chart their own futures. Or at least, we did once.

A

Some half-century ago, *Roe* struck down a state law making it a crime to perform an abortion unless its purpose was to save a woman's life. . . . The Court explained that a long line of precedents, "founded in the Fourteenth Amendment's concept of personal liberty," protected individual decisionmaking related to "marriage, procreation, contraception, family relationships, and child rearing and education." For the same reasons, the Court held, the Constitution must protect "a woman's decision whether or not to terminate her pregnancy." The Court recognized the myriad ways bearing a child can alter the "life and future" of a woman and other members of her family. A State could not, "by adopting one theory of life," override all "rights of the pregnant woman."

In the 20 years between *Roe* and *Casey*, the Court expressly reaffirmed *Roe* on two occasions, and applied it on many more. . . . Then, in *Casey*, the Court considered the matter anew, and again upheld *Roe*'s core precepts. . . . Central to that conclusion was a full-throated restatement of a woman's right to choose. Like *Roe*, *Casey* grounded that right in the Fourteenth Amendment's guarantee of "liberty." That guarantee encompasses realms of conduct not specifically referenced in the Constitution: "Marriage is mentioned nowhere" in that document, yet the Court was "no doubt correct" to protect the freedom to marry "against state interference." And the guarantee of liberty encompasses conduct today that was not protected at the time of the Fourteenth Amendment. "It is settled now," the Court said — though it was not always so — that "the Constitution places limits on a State's right to interfere with a person's most basic decisions about family and parenthood, as well as bodily integrity." . . . Especially important in this web of precedents protecting an individual's most "personal choices" were those guaranteeing the right to contraception. In those cases, the Court had recognized "the right of the individual" to make the vastly consequential "decision whether to bear" a child. So too, *Casey* reasoned, the liberty clause protects the decision of a woman confronting an unplanned pregnancy. Her decision about abortion was central, in the same way, to her capacity to chart her life's course. . . .

[The majority asserts that] *Roe* and *Casey* . . . are dismissive of a "State's interest in protecting prenatal life." Nothing could get those decisions more wrong. As just described, *Roe* and *Casey* invoked powerful state interests in that protection, operative at every stage of the pregnancy and overriding the woman's liberty after viability. The strength of those state interests is exactly why the Court allowed greater restrictions on the abortion right than on other rights deriving from the Fourteenth Amendment. But what *Roe* and *Casey* also recognized — which today's majority does not — is that a woman's freedom and equality are likewise involved. That fact — the presence of countervailing interests — is what made the abortion question hard, and what necessitated balancing. The majority scoffs at that idea, castigating us for "repeatedly prais[ing] the 'balance'" the two cases arrived at (with the word "balance" in scare quotes). To the majority "balance" is a dirty word, as moderation is a foreign concept. The majority would allow States to ban abortion from conception onward because it does not think forced childbirth at all implicates a woman's rights to equality and freedom. Today's Court, that is, does not think there is anything of constitutional significance attached to a woman's control of her body and the path of her life. *Roe* and *Casey* thought that one-sided view misguided. In some sense, that is the difference in a nutshell between our precedents and the majority opinion. The constitutional regime we have lived in for the last 50 years recognized competing interests, and sought a balance between them. The constitutional regime we enter today erases the woman's interest and recognizes only the State's (or the Federal Government's).

[T]he majority [argues] that our analogy between the right to an abortion and the rights to contraception and same-sex marriage shows that we think "[t]he Constitution does not permit the States to regard the destruction of a 'potential

life' as a matter of any significance." To the contrary. The liberty interests underlying those rights are . . . quite similar. But only in the sphere of abortion is the
state interest in protecting potential life involved. So only in that sphere, as both
Roe and *Casey* recognized, may a State impinge so far on the liberty interest
(barring abortion after viability and discouraging it before). The majority's failure to understand this fairly obvious point stems from its rejection of the idea of
balancing interests in this (or maybe in any) constitutional context. Cf. *New York
State Rifle & Pistol Assn., Inc. v. Bruen*, 597 U.S. ___, ___, ___-___ (2022) (slip
op., at 8, 15-17). The majority thinks that a woman has *no* liberty or equality
interest in the decision to bear a child, so a State's interest in protecting fetal life
necessarily prevails. (relocated footnote—eds.)

   B

   The majority makes this change based on a single question: Did the reproductive right recognized in *Roe* and *Casey* exist in "1868, the year when the
Fourteenth Amendment was ratified"? The majority says (and with this much
we agree) that the answer to this question is no: In 1868, there was no nationwide right to end a pregnancy, and no thought that the Fourteenth Amendment
provided one.
   Of course, the majority opinion refers as well to some later and earlier history. On the one side of 1868, it goes back as far as the 13th (the 13th!) century. But that turns out to be wheel-spinning. First, it is not clear what relevance
such early history should have, even to the majority. See *New York State Rifle &
Pistol Assn., Inc. v. Bruen*, 597 U.S. ___, ___ (2022) (slip op., at 26) ("Historical
evidence that long predates [ratification] may not illuminate the scope of the
right"). If the early history obviously supported abortion rights, the majority
would no doubt say that only the views of the Fourteenth Amendment's ratifiers
are germane. See *ibid.* (It is "better not to go too far back into antiquity," except
if olden "law survived to become our Founders' law"). Second—and embarrassingly for the majority—early law in fact does provide some support for abortion rights. Common-law authorities did not treat abortion as a crime before
"quickening"—the point when the fetus moved in the womb. And early American
law followed the common-law rule. . . . See J. Mohr, Abortion in America: The
Origins and Evolution of National Policy, 1800–1900, pp. 34 (1978). The majority offers no evidence to the contrary—no example of a founding-era law making prequickening abortion a crime (except when a woman died). And even in
the mid-19th century, more than 10 States continued to allow pre-quickening
abortions. See Brief for American Historical Association et al. as *Amici Curiae*
27, and n. 14. [relocated footnote—eds.]
   So the criminal law of that early time might be taken as roughly consonant
with *Roe*'s and *Casey*'s different treatment of early and late abortions. Better,
then, to move forward in time. On the other side of 1868, the majority occasionally notes that many States barred abortion up to the time of *Roe*. That is con-
venient for the majority, but it is window dressing. As the same majority (plus
one) just informed us, "post-ratification adoption or acceptance of laws that are

inconsistent with the original meaning of the constitutional text obviously cannot overcome or alter that text." *New York State Rifle & Pistol Assn., Inc.*, 597 U. S., at _____ (slip op., at 2728). Had the pre-*Roe* liberalization of abortion laws occurred more quickly and more widely in the 20th century, the majority would say (once again) that only the ratifiers' views are germane.

The majority's core legal postulate, then, is that we in the 21st century must read the Fourteenth Amendment just as its ratifiers did. And that is indeed what the majority emphasizes over and over again. See *ante*, at 47 ("[T]he most important historical fact [is] how the States regulated abortion when the Fourteenth Amendment was adopted"). If the ratifiers did not understand something as central to freedom, then neither can we. Or said more particularly: If those people did not understand reproductive rights as part of the guarantee of liberty conferred in the Fourteenth Amendment, then those rights do not exist.

As an initial matter, note a mistake in the just preceding sentence. We referred there to the "people" who ratified the Fourteenth Amendment: What rights did those "people" have in their heads at the time? But, of course, "people" did not ratify the Fourteenth Amendment. Men did. So it is perhaps not so surprising that the ratifiers were not perfectly attuned to the importance of reproductive rights for women's liberty, or for their capacity to participate as equal members of our Nation. Indeed, the ratifiers — both in 1868 and when the original Constitution was approved in 1788 — did not understand women as full members of the community embraced by the phrase "We the People." In 1868, the first wave of American feminists were explicitly told — of course by men — that it was not their time to seek constitutional protections. (Women would not get even the vote for another half-century.) To be sure, most women in 1868 also had a foreshortened view of their rights: If most men could not then imagine giving women control over their bodies, most women could not imagine having that kind of autonomy. But that takes away nothing from the core point. Those responsible for the original Constitution, including the Fourteenth Amendment, did not perceive women as equals, and did not recognize women's rights. When the majority says that we must read our foundational charter as viewed at the time of ratification (except that we may also check it against the Dark Ages), it consigns women to second-class citizenship.

Casey itself understood this point. . . It recollected with dismay a decision this Court issued just five years after the Fourteenth Amendment's ratification, approving a State's decision to deny a law license to a woman and suggesting as well that a woman had no legal status apart from her husband. [*Bradwell v. Illinois*]. "There was a time," *Casey* explained, when the Constitution did not protect "men and women alike." But times had changed. A woman's place in society had changed, and constitutional law had changed along with it. The relegation of women to inferior status in either the public sphere or the family was "no longer consistent with our understanding" of the Constitution. Now, "[t]he Constitution protects all individuals, male or female," from "the abuse of governmental power" or "unjustified state interference."

So how is it that, as *Casey* said, our Constitution, read now, grants rights to women, though it did not in 1868? How is it that our Constitution subjects discrimination against them to heightened judicial scrutiny? How is it that our Constitution, through the Fourteenth Amendment's liberty clause, guarantees access to contraception (also not legally protected in 1868) so that women can decide for themselves whether and when to bear a child? How is it that until today, that same constitutional clause protected a woman's right, in the event contraception failed, to end a pregnancy in its earlier stages?

The answer is that this Court has rejected the majority's pinched view of how to read our Constitution. "The Founders," we recently wrote, "knew they were writing a document designed to apply to ever-changing circumstances over centuries." Or in the words of the great Chief Justice John Marshall, our Constitution is "intended to endure for ages to come," and must adapt itself to a future "seen dimly," if at all. *McCulloch v. Maryland*, 4 Wheat. 316, 415 (1819). That is indeed why our Constitution is written as it is. The Framers (both in 1788 and 1868) understood that the world changes. So they did not define rights by reference to the specific practices existing at the time. Instead, the Framers defined rights in general terms, to permit future evolution in their scope and meaning. And over the course of our history, this Court has taken up the Framers' invitation. It has kept true to the Framers' principles by applying them in new ways, responsive to new societal understandings and conditions.

Nowhere has that approach been more prevalent than in construing the majestic but open-ended words of the Fourteenth Amendment — the guarantees of "liberty" and "equality" for all. And nowhere has that approach produced prouder moments, for this country and the Court. Consider an example *Obergefell* used a few years ago. The Court there confronted a claim, based on *Washington v. Glucksberg*, 521 U.S. 702 (1997), that the Fourteenth Amendment "must be defined in a most circumscribed manner, with central reference to specific historical practices" — exactly the view today's majority follows. And the Court specifically rejected that view.

. . . The majority ignores that rejection. But it is unequivocal: The *Glucksberg* test, *Obergefell* said, "may have been appropriate" in considering physician-assisted suicide, but "is inconsistent with the approach this Court has used in discussing other fundamental rights, including marriage and intimacy." [relocated footnote — eds.]

In [rejecting *Glucksberg*'s focus on specific historical practices], the Court reflected on what the proposed, historically circumscribed approach would have meant for interracial marriage. The Fourteenth Amendment's ratifiers did not think it gave black and white people a right to marry each other. To the contrary, contemporaneous practice deemed that act quite as unprotected as abortion. Yet the Court in *Loving v. Virginia*, 388 U.S. 1 (1967), read the Fourteenth Amendment to embrace the Lovings' union. If, *Obergefell* explained, "rights were defined by who exercised them in the past, then received practices could serve as their own continued justification" — even when they conflict with "liberty" and "equality" as later and more broadly understood. The Constitution does not freeze for all time the original view of what those rights guarantee, or how they apply.

That does not mean anything goes. The majority wishes people to think there are but two alternatives: (1) accept the original applications of the Fourteenth Amendment and no others, or (2) surrender to judges' "own ardent views," ungrounded in law, about the "liberty that Americans should enjoy." At least, that idea is what the majority *sometimes* tries to convey. At other times, the majority (or, rather, most of it) tries to assure the public that it has no designs on rights (for example, to contraception) that arose only in the back half of the 20th century—in other words, that it is happy to pick and choose, in accord with individual preferences.

[O]ur point is . . . that applications of liberty and equality can evolve while remaining grounded in constitutional principles, constitutional history, and constitutional precedents. The second Justice Harlan discussed how to strike the right balance when he explained why he would have invalidated a State's ban on contraceptive use. Judges, he said, are not "free to roam where unguided speculation might take them." *Poe v. Ullman*, 367 U.S. 497, 542 (1961) (dissenting opinion). Yet they also must recognize that the constitutional "tradition" of this country is not captured whole at a single moment. Rather, its meaning gains content from the long sweep of our history and from successive judicial precedents—each looking to the last and each seeking to apply the Constitution's most fundamental commitments to new conditions. That is why Americans, to go back to *Obergefell*'s example, have a right to marry across racial lines. And it is why, to go back to Justice Harlan's case, Americans have a right to use contraceptives so they can choose for themselves whether to have children.

. . . *Casey* explicitly rejected the present majority's method. "[T]he specific practices of States at the time of the adoption of the Fourteenth Amendment," *Casey* stated, do not "mark[] the outer limits of the substantive sphere of liberty which the Fourteenth Amendment protects." To hold otherwise—as the majority does today—"would be inconsistent with our law." Why? Because the Court has "vindicated [the] principle" over and over that (no matter the sentiment in 1868) "there is a realm of personal liberty which the government may not enter"—especially relating to "bodily integrity" and "family life." *Casey* described in detail the Court's contraception cases. It noted decisions protecting the right to marry, including to someone of another race. In reviewing decades and decades of constitutional law, *Casey* could draw but one conclusion: Whatever was true in 1868, "[i]t is settled now, as it was when the Court heard arguments in *Roe v. Wade*, that the Constitution places limits on a State's right to interfere with a person's most basic decisions about family and parenthood."

And that conclusion still held good, until the Court's intervention here. It was settled at the time of *Roe*, settled at the time of *Casey*, and settled yesterday that the Constitution places limits on a State's power to assert control over an individual's body and most personal decisionmaking. A multitude of decisions supporting that principle led to *Roe*'s recognition and *Casey*'s reaffirmation of the right to choose; and *Roe* and *Casey* in turn supported additional protections for intimate and familial relations. The majority has embarrassingly little to say about those precedents. It (literally) rattles them off in a single paragraph; and it implies that they have nothing to do with each other, or with the right to terminate an early pregnancy. . . . But that is flat wrong. The Court's precedents about bodily autonomy, sexual and familial relations, and procreation are all interwoven—all part of the fabric of our constitutional law, and because that is so, of our lives. Especially women's lives, where they safeguard a right to self-determination.

And eliminating that right, we need to say before further describing our precedents, is not taking a "neutral" position, as JUSTICE KAVANAUGH tries to argue. His idea is that neutrality lies in giving the abortion issue to the States, where some can go one way and some another. But would he say that the Court is being "scrupulously neutral" if it allowed New York and California to ban all the guns they want? If the Court allowed some States to use unanimous juries and others not? If the Court told the States: Decide for yourselves whether to put restrictions on church attendance? We could go on—and in fact we will. Suppose JUSTICE KAVANAUGH were to say (in line with the majority opinion) that the rights we just listed are more textually or historically grounded than the right to choose. What, then, of the right to contraception or same-sex marriage? Would it be "scrupulously neutral" for the Court to eliminate those rights too? The point of all these examples is that when it comes to rights, the Court does not act "neutrally" when it leaves everything up to the States. Rather, the Court acts neutrally when it protects the right against all comers. And to apply that point to the case here: When the Court decimates a right women have held for 50 years, the Court is not being "scrupulously neutral." It is instead taking sides: against women who wish to exercise the right, and for States (like Mississippi) that want to bar them from doing so. JUSTICE KAVANAUGH cannot obscure that point by appropriating the rhetoric of even-handedness. His position just is what it is: A brook-no-compromise refusal to recognize a woman's right to choose, from the first day of a pregnancy. And that position, as we will now show, cannot be squared with this Court's longstanding view that women indeed have rights (whatever the state of the world in 1868) to make the most personal and consequential decisions about their bodies and their lives.

Consider first, then, the line of this Court's cases protecting "bodily integrity." *Casey*. "No right," in this Court's time-honored view, "is held more sacred, or is more carefully guarded," than "the right of every individual to the possession and control of his own person."*Union Pacific R. Co. v. Botsford*, 141 U.S. 250, 251 (1891); see *Cruzan v. Director, Mo. Dept. of Health*, 497 U.S. 261, 269 (1990) (Every adult "has a right to determine what shall be done with his own body"). Or to put it more simply: Everyone, including women, owns their own bodies. So the Court has restricted the power of government to interfere with a person's medical decisions or compel her to undergo medical procedures or treatments. See, *e.g.*, *Winston v. Lee*, 470 U.S. 753, 766-767 (1985) (forced surgery); *Rochin v. California*, 342 U.S. 165, 166, 173-174 (1952) (forced stomach pumping); *Washington v. Harper*, 494 U.S. 210, 229, 236 (1990) (forced administration of antipsychotic drugs).

Casey recognized the "doctrinal affinity" between those precedents and *Roe*. And that doctrinal affinity is born of a factual likeness. There are few greater incursions on a body than forcing a woman to complete a pregnancy and give birth. For every woman, those experiences involve all manner of physical changes, medical treatments (including the possibility of a cesarean section), and medical risk. Just as one example, an American woman is 14 times more likely to die by carrying a pregnancy to term than by having an abortion. That women happily undergo those burdens and hazards of their own accord does not lessen how far a State impinges on a woman's body when it compels her to bring a pregnancy to term. And for some women, as *Roe* recognized, abortions are medically necessary to prevent harm. The majority does not say — which is itself ominous — whether a State may prevent a woman from obtaining an abortion when she and her doctor have determined it is a needed medical treatment.

So too, *Roe* and *Casey* fit neatly into a long line of decisions protecting from government intrusion a wealth of private choices about family matters, child rearing, intimate relationships, and procreation. Those cases safeguard particular choices about whom to marry; whom to have sex with; what family members to live with; how to raise children — and crucially, whether and when to have children. In varied cases, the Court explained that those choices — "the most intimate and personal" a person can make — reflect fundamental aspects of personal identity; they define the very "attributes of personhood." *Casey*. And they inevitably shape the nature and future course of a person's life (and often the lives of those closest to her). So, the Court held, those choices belong to the individual, and not the government. That is the essence of what liberty requires.

And liberty may require it, this Court has repeatedly said, even when those living in 1868 would not have recognized the claim — because they would not have seen the person making it as a full-fledged member of the community. Throughout our history, the sphere of protected liberty has expanded, bringing in individuals formerly excluded. In that way, the constitutional values of liberty and equality go hand in hand; they do not inhabit the hermetically sealed containers the majority portrays. So before *Roe* and *Casey*, the Court expanded in successive cases those who could claim the right to marry — though their relationships would have been outside the law's protection in the mid-19th century. See, *e.g.*, *Loving*, 388 U.S. 1 (interracial couples); *Turner v. Safley*, 482 U.S. 78 (1987) (prisoners); see also, *e.g.*, *Stanley v. Illinois*, 405 U.S. 645, 651-652 (1972) (offering constitutional protection to untraditional "family unit[s]"). And after *Roe* and *Casey*, of course, the Court continued in that vein. With a critical stop to hold that the Fourteenth Amendment protected same-sex intimacy, the Court resolved that the Amendment also conferred on same-sex couples the right to marry. See *Lawrence*; *Obergefell*. In considering that question, the Court held, "[h]istory and tradition," especially as reflected in the course of our precedent, "guide and discipline [the] inquiry." But the sentiments of 1868 alone do not and cannot "rule the present."

Casey similarly recognized the need to extend the constitutional sphere of liberty to a previously excluded group. The Court then understood, as the majority today does not, that the men who ratified the Fourteenth Amendment and wrote the state laws of the time did not view women as full and equal citizens. A woman then, Casey wrote, "had no legal existence separate from her husband." Women were seen only "as the center of home and family life," without "full and independent legal status under the Constitution." But that could not be true any longer: The State could not now insist on the historically dominant "vision of the woman's role." And equal citizenship, Casey realized, was inescapably connected to reproductive rights. "The ability of women to participate equally" in the "life of the Nation"—in all its economic, social, political, and legal aspects—"has been facilitated by their ability to control their reproductive lives." Without the ability to decide whether and when to have children, women could not—in the way men took for granted—determine how they would live their lives, and how they would contribute to the society around them.

For much that reason, Casey made clear that the precedents Roe most closely tracked were those involving contraception. Over the course of three cases, the Court had held that a right to use and gain access to contraception was part of the Fourteenth Amendment's guarantee of liberty. See Griswold; Eisenstadt; Carey v. Population Services Int'l, 431 U.S. 678 (1977). That clause, we explained, necessarily conferred a right "to be free from unwarranted governmental intrusion into matters so fundamentally affecting a person as the decision whether to bear or beget a child." Eisenstadt. Casey saw Roe as of a piece: In "critical respects the abortion decision is of the same character." "[R]easonable people," the Court noted, could also oppose contraception; and indeed, they could believe that "some forms of contraception" similarly implicate a concern with "potential life." Yet the views of others could not automatically prevail against a woman's right to control her own body and make her own choice about whether to bear, and probably to raise, a child. When an unplanned pregnancy is involved—because either contraception or abortion is outlawed—"the liberty of the woman is at stake in a sense unique to the human condition." No State could undertake to resolve the moral questions raised "in such a definitive way" as to deprive a woman of all choice.

Faced with all these connections between Roe/Casey and judicial decisions recognizing other constitutional rights, the majority tells everyone not to worry. It can (so it says) neatly extract the right to choose from the constitutional edifice without affecting any associated rights. (Think of someone telling you that the Jenga tower simply will not collapse.) Today's decision, the majority first says, "does not undermine" the decisions cited by Roe and Casey—the ones involving "marriage, procreation, contraception, [and] family relationships"—"in any way." Note that this first assurance does not extend to rights recognized after Roe and Casey, and partly based on them—in particular, rights to same-sex intimacy and marriage. On its later tries, though, the majority includes those too: "Nothing in this opinion should be understood to cast doubt on precedents that do not concern abortion." That right is unique, the majority asserts, "because [abortion] terminates life or potential life." So the majority depicts today's decision as "a restricted railroad ticket, good for this day and train only." *Smith v. Allwright*, 321 U.S. 649, 669 (1944) (Roberts, J., dissenting). Should the audience for these too-much-repeated protestations be duly satisfied? We think not.

The first problem with the majority's account comes from JUSTICE THOMAS's concurrence—which makes clear he is not with the program. In saying that nothing in today's opinion casts doubt on non-abortion precedents, JUSTICE THOMAS explains, he means only that they are not at issue in this very case. But he lets us know what he wants to do when they are. "[I]n future cases," he says, "we should reconsider all of this Court's substantive due process precedents, including *Griswold*, *Lawrence*, and *Obergefell*." And when we reconsider them? Then "we have a duty" to "overrul[e] these demonstrably erroneous decisions." So at least one Justice is planning to use the ticket of today's decision again and again and again.

Even placing the concurrence to the side, the assurance in today's opinion still does not work. Or at least that is so if the majority is serious about its sole reason for overturning *Roe* and *Casey*: the legal status of abortion in the 19th century. Except in the places quoted above, the state interest in protecting fetal life plays no part in the majority's analysis. To the contrary, the majority takes pride in not expressing a view "about the status of the fetus." The majority's departure from *Roe* and *Casey* rests instead—and only—on whether a woman's decision to end a pregnancy involves any Fourteenth Amendment liberty interest (against which *Roe* and *Casey* balanced the state interest in preserving fetal life). According to the majority, no liberty interest is present—because (and only because) the law offered no protection to the woman's choice in the 19th century. But here is the rub. The law also did not then (and would not for ages) protect a wealth of other things. It did not protect the rights recognized in *Lawrence* and *Obergefell* to same-sex intimacy and marriage. It did not protect the right recognized in *Loving* to marry across racial lines. It did not protect the right recognized in *Griswold* to contraceptive use. For that matter, it did not protect the right recognized in *Skinner v. Oklahoma ex rel. Williamson*, 316 U.S. 535 (1942), not to be sterilized without consent. So if the majority is right in its legal analysis, all those decisions were wrong, and all those matters properly belong to the States too—whatever the particular state interests involved. And if that is true, it is impossible to understand (as a matter of logic and principle) how the majority can say that its opinion today does not threaten—does not even "undermine"—any number of other constitutional rights.

Nor does it even help just to take the majority at its word. Assume the majority is sincere in saying, for whatever reason, that it will go so far and no further. Scout's honor. Still, the future significance of today's opinion will be decided in the future. And law often has a way of evolving without regard to original intentions — a way of actually following where logic leads, rather than tolerating hard-to-explain lines. Rights can expand in that way. Dissenting in *Lawrence*, Justice Scalia explained why he took no comfort in the Court's statement that a decision recognizing the right to same-sex intimacy did "not involve" same-sex marriage. That could be true, he wrote, "only if one entertains the belief that principle and logic have nothing to do with the decisions of this Court." Score one for the dissent, as a matter of prophecy. And logic and principle are not one-way ratchets. Rights can contract in the same way and for the same reason — because whatever today's majority might say, one thing really does lead to another. We fervently hope that does not happen because of today's decision. We hope that we will not join Justice Scalia in the book of prophets. But we cannot understand how anyone can be confident that today's opinion will be the last of its kind.

Consider, as our last word on this issue, contraception. The Constitution, of course, does not mention that word. And there is no historical right to contraception, of the kind the majority insists on. To the contrary, the American legal landscape in the decades after the Civil War was littered with bans on the sale of contraceptive devices. So again, there seem to be two choices. If the majority is serious about its historical approach, then *Griswold* and its progeny are in the line of fire too. Or if it is not serious, then . . . what *is* the basis of today's decision? If we had to guess, we suspect the prospects of this Court approving bans on contraception are low. But once again, the future significance of today's opinion will be decided in the future. At the least, today's opinion will fuel the fight to get contraception, and any other issues with a moral dimension, out of the Fourteenth Amendment and into state legislatures.

Anyway, today's decision, taken on its own, is catastrophic enough. As a matter of constitutional method, the majority's commitment to replicate in 2022 every view about the meaning of liberty held in 1868 has precious little to recommend it. Our law in this constitutional sphere, as in most, has for decades upon decades proceeded differently. It has considered fundamental constitutional principles, the whole course of the Nation's history and traditions, and the step-by-step evolution of the Court's precedents. It is disciplined but not static. It relies on accumulated judgments, not just the sentiments of one long-ago generation of men (who themselves believed, and drafted the Constitution to reflect, that the world progresses). And by doing so, it includes those excluded from that olden conversation, rather than perpetuating its bounds.

As a matter of constitutional substance, the majority's opinion has all the flaws its method would suggest. Because laws in 1868 deprived women of any control over their bodies, the majority approves States doing so today. Because those laws prevented women from charting the course of their own lives, the majority says States can do the same again. Because in 1868, the government could tell a pregnant woman — even in the first days of her pregnancy — that she could do nothing but bear a child, it can once more impose that command. Today's decision strips women of agency over what even the majority agrees is a contested and contestable moral issue. It forces her to carry out the State's will, whatever the circumstances and whatever the harm it will wreak on her and her family. In the Fourteenth Amendment's terms, it takes away her liberty. Even before we get to *stare decisis*, we dissent.

II

By overruling *Roe*, *Casey*, and more than 20 cases reaffirming or applying the constitutional right to abortion, the majority abandons *stare decisis*, a principle central to the rule of law. . . . *Stare decisis* "promotes the evenhanded, predictable, and consistent development of legal principles." It maintains a stability that allows people to order their lives under the law. *Stare decisis* also "contributes to the integrity of our constitutional system of government" by ensuring that decisions "are founded in the law rather than in the proclivities of individuals." As Hamilton wrote: It "avoid[s] an arbitrary discretion in the courts." The Federalist No. 78. And as Blackstone said before him: It "keep[s] the scale of justice even and steady, and not liable to waver with every new judge's opinion.". . .

[T]he Court may not overrule a decision, even a constitutional one, without a "special justification." *Stare decisis* is, of course, not an "inexorable command"; it is sometimes appropriate to overrule an earlier decision. But the Court must have a good reason to do so over and above the belief "that the precedent was wrongly decided." "[I]t is not alone sufficient that we would decide a case differently now than we did then."

The majority today lists some 30 of our cases as overruling precedent, and argues that they support overruling *Roe* and *Casey*. But none does. . . In some, the Court only partially modified or clarified a precedent. And in the rest, the Court relied on one or more of the traditional *stare decisis* factors in reaching its conclusion. The Court found, for example, (1) a change in legal doctrine that undermined or made obsolete the earlier decision; (2) a factual change that had the same effect; or (3) an absence of reliance because the earlier decision was less than a decade old. (The majority is wrong when it says that we insist on a test of changed law or fact alone, although that is present in most of the cases.)

None of those factors apply here: Nothing—and in particular, no significant legal or factual change—supports overturning a half-century of settled law giving women control over their reproductive lives. First, for all the reasons we have given, *Roe* and *Casey* were correct. . . . [T]he Court protected women's liberty and women's equality in a way comporting with our Fourteenth Amendment precedents. . . .

In any event "[w]hether or not we . . . agree" with a prior precedent is the beginning, not the end, of our analysis—and the remaining "principles of *stare decisis* weigh heavily against overruling" *Roe* and *Casey*. . . . No changes in either law or fact have eroded the two decisions. And tens of millions of American women have relied, and continue to rely, on the right to choose. So under traditional *stare decisis* principles, the majority has no special justification for the harm it causes.

[T]he majority barely mentions any legal or factual changes that have occurred since *Roe* and *Casey*. It suggests that the two decisions are hard for courts to implement, but cannot prove its case. In the end, the majority says, all it must say to override *stare decisis* is one thing: that it believes *Roe* and *Casey* "egregiously wrong." That rule could equally spell the end of any precedent with which a bare majority of the present Court disagrees. . . . It makes radical change too easy and too fast, based on nothing more than the new views of new judges. The majority has overruled *Roe* and *Casey* for one and only one reason: because it has always despised them, and now it has the votes to discard them. The majority thereby substitutes a rule by judges for the rule of law.

A

Contrary to the majority's view, there is nothing unworkable about *Casey*'s "undue burden" standard. Its primary focus on whether a State has placed a "substantial obstacle" on a woman seeking an abortion is "the sort of inquiry familiar to judges across a variety of contexts." And it has given rise to no more conflict in application than many standards this Court and others unhesitatingly apply every day. . . . The *Casey* undue burden standard . . . resembles general standards that courts work with daily in other legal spheres—like the "rule of reason" in antitrust law or the "arbitrary and capricious" standard for agency decisionmaking. Applying general standards to particular cases is, in many contexts, just what it means to do law.

Anyone concerned about workability should consider the majority's substitute standard. The majority says a law regulating or banning abortion "must be sustained if there is a rational basis on which the legislature could have thought that it would serve legitimate state interests." And the majority lists interests like "respect for and preservation of prenatal life," "protection of maternal health," elimination of certain "medical procedures," "mitigation of fetal pain," and others. This Court will surely face critical questions about how that test applies. Must a state law allow abortions when necessary to protect a woman's life and health? And if so, exactly when? How much risk to a woman's life can a State force her to incur, before the Fourteenth Amendment's protection of life kicks in? Suppose a patient with pulmonary hypertension has a 30-to-50 percent risk of dying with ongoing pregnancy; is that enough? And short of death, how much illness or injury can the State require her to accept, consistent with the Amendment's protection of liberty and equality? Further, the Court may face questions about the application of abortion regulations to medical care most people view as quite different from abortion. What about the morning-after pill? IUDs? In vitro fertilization? And how about the use of dilation and evacuation or medication for miscarriage management? . . . To take just the last, most medical treatments for miscarriage are identical to those used in abortions. Blanket restrictions on "abortion" procedures and medications therefore may be understood to deprive women of effective treatment for miscarriages, which occur in about 10 to 30 percent of pregnancies. [relocated footnote—eds.]

Finally, the majority's ruling today invites a host of questions about interstate conflicts. Can a State bar women from traveling to another State to obtain an abortion? Can a State prohibit advertising out-of-state abortions or helping women get to out-of-state providers? Can a State interfere with the mailing of drugs used for medication abortions? The Constitution protects travel and speech and interstate commerce, so today's ruling will give rise to a host of new constitutional questions. Far from removing the Court from the abortion issue, the majority puts the Court at the center of the coming "interjurisdictional abortion wars."

In short, the majority does not save judges from unwieldy tests or extricate them from the sphere of controversy. To the contrary, it discards a known, workable, and predictable standard in favor of something novel and probably far more complicated. It forces the Court to wade further into hotly contested issues, including moral and philosophical ones, that the majority criticizes *Roe* and *Casey* for addressing.

B

When overruling constitutional precedent, the Court has almost always pointed to major legal or factual changes undermining a decision's original basis. . . . But it is not so today. . . . The majority briefly invokes the current controversy over abortion. But it has to acknowledge that the same dispute has existed for decades: Conflict over abortion is not a change but a constant. . . . In the end, the majority throws longstanding precedent to the winds without showing that anything significant has changed to justify its radical reshaping of the law.

[N]o subsequent factual developments have undermined *Roe* and *Casey*. Women continue to experience unplanned pregnancies and unexpected developments in pregnancies. Pregnancies continue to have enormous physical, social, and economic consequences. Even an uncomplicated pregnancy imposes significant strain on the body, unavoidably involving significant physiological change and excruciating pain. For some women, pregnancy and childbirth can mean life-altering physical ailments or even death. Today, as noted earlier, the risks of carrying a pregnancy to term dwarf those of having an abortion. . . . The majority briefly refers to arguments about changes in laws relating to healthcare coverage, pregnancy discrimination, and family leave. Many women, however, still do not have adequate healthcare coverage before and after pregnancy; and, even when insurance coverage is available, healthcare services may be far away. Women also continue to face pregnancy discrimination that interferes with their ability to earn a living. Paid family leave remains inaccessible to many who need it most. Only 20 percent of private-sector workers have access to paid family leave, including a mere 8 percent of workers in the bottom quartile of wage earners.

The majority briefly notes the growing prevalence of safe haven laws and demand for adoption, but, to the degree that these are changes at all, they too are irrelevant. Neither reduces the health risks or financial costs of going through pregnancy and childbirth. Moreover, the choice to give up parental rights after giving birth is altogether different from the choice not to carry a pregnancy to term. The reality is that few women denied an abortion will choose adoption. . . . A study of women who sought an abortion but were denied one because of gestational limits found that only 9 percent put the child up for adoption, rather than parenting themselves. See G. Sisson, L. Ralph, H. Gould, & D. Foster, Adoption Decision Making Among Women Seeking Abortion, 27 Women's Health Issues 136, 139 (2017). [relocated footnote — eds.] . . . The vast majority will continue, just as in *Roe* and *Casey*'s time, to shoulder the costs of childrearing. Whether or not they choose to parent, they will experience the profound loss of autonomy and dignity that coerced pregnancy and birth always impose.

Mississippi's own record illustrates how little facts on the ground have changed since *Roe* and *Casey*, notwithstanding the majority's supposed "modern developments." Sixty-two percent of pregnancies in Mississippi are unplanned, yet Mississippi does not require insurance to cover contraceptives and prohibits educators from demonstrating proper contraceptive use. The State neither bans pregnancy discrimination nor requires provision of paid parental leave. It has strict eligibility requirements for Medicaid and nutrition assistance, leaving many women and families without basic medical care or enough food. Although 86 percent of pregnancy-related deaths in the State are due to postpartum complications, Mississippi rejected federal funding to provide a year's worth of Medicaid coverage to women after giving birth. Perhaps unsurprisingly, health outcomes in Mississippi are abysmal for both women and children. Mississippi has the highest infant mortality rate in the country, and some of the highest rates for preterm birth, low birthweight, cesarean section, and maternal death. It is approximately 75 times more dangerous for a woman in the State to carry a pregnancy to term than to have an abortion. We do not say that every State is Mississippi, and we are sure some have made gains since *Roe* and *Casey* in providing support for women and children. But a state-by-state analysis by public health professionals shows that States with the most restrictive abortion policies also continue to invest the least in women's and children's health.

The only notable change we can see since *Roe* and *Casey* cuts in favor of adhering to precedent: It is that American abortion law has become more and more aligned with other nations. The majority, like the Mississippi Legislature, claims that the United States is an extreme outlier when it comes to abortion regulation. The global trend, however, has been toward increased provision of legal and safe abortion care. A number of countries, including New Zealand, the Netherlands, and Iceland, permit abortions up to a roughly similar time as *Roe* and *Casey* set. Canada has decriminalized abortion at any point in a pregnancy. Most Western European countries impose restrictions on abortion after 12 to 14 weeks, but they often have liberal exceptions to those time limits, including to prevent harm to a woman's physical or mental health. They also typically make access to early abortion easier, for example, by helping cover its cost. Perhaps most notable, more than 50 countries around the world — in Asia, Latin America, Africa, and Europe — have expanded access to abortion in the past 25 years. In light of that worldwide liberalization of abortion laws, it is American States that will become international outliers after today.

In sum, the majority can point to neither legal nor factual developments in support of its decision. Nothing that has happened in this country or the world in recent decades undermines the core insight of *Roe* and *Casey*. It continues to be true that, within the constraints those decisions established, a woman, not the government, should choose whether she will bear the burdens of pregnancy, childbirth, and parenting. . . .

C

The reasons for retaining *Roe* and *Casey* gain further strength from the overwhelming reliance interests those decisions have created. The Court adheres to precedent not just for institutional reasons, but because it recognizes that stability in the law is "an essential thread in the mantle of protection that the law affords the individual." So when overruling precedent "would dislodge [individuals'] settled rights and expectations," *stare decisis* has "added force." *Casey* understood that to deny individuals' reliance on *Roe* was to "refuse to face the fact[s]." Today the majority refuses to face the facts. "The most striking feature of the [majority] is the absence of any serious discussion" of how its ruling will affect women. By characterizing *Casey*'s reliance arguments as "generalized assertions about the national psyche," it reveals how little it knows or cares about women's lives or about the suffering its decision will cause.

In *Casey*, the Court observed that for two decades individuals "have organized intimate relationships and made" significant life choices "in reliance on the availability of abortion in the event that contraception should fail." Over another 30 years, that reliance has solidified. For half a century now, in *Casey*'s words, "[t]he ability of women to participate equally in the economic and social life of the Nation has been facilitated by their ability to control their reproductive lives." Indeed, all women now of childbearing age have grown up expecting that they would be able to avail themselves of *Roe*'s and *Casey*'s protections.

The disruption of overturning *Roe* and *Casey* will therefore be profound. Abortion is a common medical procedure and a familiar experience in women's lives. About 18 percent of pregnancies in this country end in abortion, and about one quarter of American women will have an abortion before the age of 45. Those numbers reflect the predictable and life-changing effects of carrying a pregnancy, giving birth, and becoming a parent. As *Casey* understood, people today rely on their ability to control and time pregnancies when making countless life decisions: where to live, whether and how to invest in education or careers, how to allocate financial resources, and how to approach intimate and family relationships. Women may count on abortion access for when contraception fails. They may count on abortion access for when contraception cannot be used, for example, if they were raped. They may count on abortion for when something changes in the midst of a pregnancy, whether it involves family or financial circumstances, unanticipated medical complications, or heartbreaking fetal diagnoses. Taking away the right to abortion, as the majority does today, destroys all those individual plans and expectations. In so doing, it diminishes women's opportunities to participate fully and equally in the Nation's political, social, and economic life.

The majority's response to these obvious points exists far from the reality American women actually live. The majority proclaims that " 'reproductive planning could take virtually immediate account of any sudden restoration of state authority to ban abortions.' " The facts are: 45 percent of pregnancies in the United States are unplanned. Even the most effective contraceptives fail, and effective contraceptives are not universally accessible. Not all sexual activity is consensual and not all contraceptive choices are made by the party who risks pregnancy. The Mississippi law at issue here, for example, has no exception for rape or incest, even for underage women. Finally, the majority ignores, as explained above, that some women decide to have an abortion because their circumstances change during a pregnancy. Human bodies care little for hopes and plans. Events can occur after conception, from unexpected medical risks to changes in family circumstances, which profoundly alter what it means to carry a pregnancy to term. In all these situations, women have expected that they will get to decide, perhaps in consultation with their families or doctors but free from state interference, whether to continue a pregnancy. For those who will now have to undergo that pregnancy, the loss of *Roe* and *Casey* could be disastrous.

That is especially so for women without money. When we "count[] the cost of [*Roe*'s] repudiation" on women who once relied on that decision, it is not hard to see where the greatest burden will fall. In States that bar abortion, women of means will still be able to travel to obtain the services they need. It is women who cannot afford to do so who will suffer most. These are the women most likely to seek abortion care in the first place. Women living below the federal poverty line experience unintended pregnancies at rates five times higher than higher income women do, and nearly half of women who seek abortion care live in households below the poverty line. Even with *Roe*'s protection, these women face immense obstacles to raising the money needed to obtain abortion care early in their pregnancy. After today, in States where legal abortions are not available, they will lose any ability to obtain safe, legal abortion care. They will not have the money to make the trip necessary; or to obtain childcare for that time; or to take time off work. Many will endure the costs and risks of pregnancy and giving birth against their wishes. Others will turn in desperation to illegal and unsafe abortions. They may lose not just their freedom, but their lives.

Finally, the expectation of reproductive control is integral to many women's identity and their place in the Nation. That expectation helps define a woman as an "equal citizen[]," with all the rights, privileges, and obligations that status entails. It reflects that she is an autonomous person, and that society and the law recognize her as such. Like many constitutional rights, the right to choose situates a woman in relationship to others and to the government. It helps define a sphere of freedom, in which a person has the capacity to make choices free of government control. As *Casey* recognized, the right "order[s]" her "thinking" as well as her "living." Beyond any individual choice about residence, or education, or career, her whole life reflects the control and authority that the right grants.

Withdrawing a woman's right to choose whether to continue a pregnancy does not mean that no choice is being made. It means that a majority of today's Court has wrenched this choice from women and given it to the States. To allow a State to exert control over one of "the most intimate and personal choices" a woman may make is not only to affect the course of her life, monumental as those effects might be. It is to alter her "views of [herself]" and her understanding of her "place[] in society" as someone with the recognized dignity and authority to make these choices. Women have relied on *Roe* and *Casey* in this way for 50 years. Many have never known anything else. When *Roe* and *Casey* disappear, the loss of power, control, and dignity will be immense.

The Court's failure to perceive the whole swath of expectations *Roe* and *Casey* created reflects an impoverished view of reliance. According to the majority, a reliance interest must be "very concrete," like those involving "property" or "contract." While many of this Court's cases addressing reliance have been in the "commercial context," none holds that interests must be analogous to commercial ones to warrant *stare decisis* protection. This unprecedented assertion is, at bottom, a radical claim to power. By disclaiming any need to consider broad swaths of individuals' interests, the Court arrogates to itself the authority to overrule established legal principles without even acknowledging the costs of its decisions for the individuals who live under the law, costs that this Court's *stare decisis* doctrine instructs us to privilege when deciding whether to change course.

The majority claims that the reliance interests women have in *Roe* and *Casey* are too "intangible" for the Court to consider, even if it were inclined to do so. This is to ignore as judges what we know as men and women. The interests women have in *Roe* and *Casey* are perfectly, viscerally concrete. Countless women will now make different decisions about careers, education, relationships, and whether to try to become pregnant than they would have when *Roe* served as a backstop. Other women will carry pregnancies to term, with all the costs and risk of harm that involves, when they would previously have chosen to obtain an abortion. For millions of women, *Roe* and *Casey* have been critical in giving them control of their bodies and their lives. Closing our eyes to the suffering today's decision will impose will not make that suffering disappear. The majority cannot escape its obligation to "count[] the cost[s]" of its decision by invoking the "conflicting arguments" of "contending sides." *Stare decisis* requires that the Court calculate the costs of a decision's repudiation on those who have relied on the decision, not on those who have disavowed it.

More broadly, the majority's approach to reliance cannot be reconciled with our Nation's understanding of constitutional rights. The majority's insistence on a "concrete," economic showing would preclude a finding of reliance on a wide variety of decisions recognizing constitutional rights—such as the right to express opinions, or choose whom to marry, or decide how to educate children. The Court, on the majority's logic, could transfer those choices to the State without having to consider a person's settled understanding that the law makes them hers. That must be wrong. All those rights, like the right to obtain an abortion, profoundly affect and, indeed, anchor individual lives. To recognize that people have relied on these rights is not to dabble in abstractions, but to acknowledge some of the most "concrete" and familiar aspects of human life and liberty. . . .

After today, young women will come of age with fewer rights than their mothers and grandmothers had. The majority accomplishes that result without so much as considering how women have relied on the right to choose or what it means to take that right away. The majority's refusal even to consider the life-altering consequences of reversing *Roe* and *Casey* is a stunning indictment of its decision. . . .

With sorrow—for this Court, but more, for the many millions of American women who have today lost a fundamental constitutional protection—we dissent.

Discussion

1. *What is the test for fundamental rights? The return of* Glucksberg. Justice Alito's opinion in *Dobbs* employs arguments made by the dissenting Justices in *Obergefell v. Hodges*. He takes his test for fundamental rights under the Due Process Clause from *Washington v. Glucksberg*, 521 U.S. 702 (1997). According to this approach, one must engage in a "careful description" of what right is at stake and one must show that this right is "deeply rooted in this Nation's history and tradition" and "implicit in the concept of ordered liberty." If a right is not "deeply rooted in this Nation's history and tradition," it is irrelevant that it is otherwise very important. To decide whether a right is deeply rooted, Alito argues that we must look to whether there is a long history of protecting the specific right at issue—in this case, the right to abortion—and he concludes that there is not. (The debate over what history shows is discussed in note 2, *infra*).

It is important to note, however, that *Glucksberg* was decided only five years after the Court had just reaffirmed *Roe* in *Casey*. Justice Kennedy, the co-author of *Casey*, was in the majority, and Chief Justice Rehnquist's majority opinion cited *Casey* as an example of a decision consistent with its approach. See 520 U.S. at 720, 726-28.

In *Dobbs*, by contrast, Justice Alito invokes *Glucksberg* without ever mentioning that it recognized abortion as a protected liberty. He appeals to *Glucksberg*'s history and traditions test as authority to argue that because abortion was banned in the past, it is not protected by the Due Process Clause.

In general the *Glucksberg* test has been favored by the Court's conservatives, but it has not been adopted by the Court's liberals. For example, the Court refused to follow *Glucksberg*'s approach in either of the substantive due process cases that followed it, *Lawrence v. Texas* and *Obergefell v. Hodges*.

In fact, Justice Kennedy's opinion in *Obergefell* specifically rejected the approach that Alito takes in *Dobbs*. Kennedy explained that the claim that liberty "must be defined in a most circumscribed manner, with central reference to specific historical practices . . . may have been appropriate for the asserted right [in *Glucksberg*] (physician-assisted suicide), [but] it is inconsistent with the approach this Court has used in discussing other fundamental rights, including marriage and intimacy. . . . If rights were defined by who exercised them in the past, then received practices could serve as their own continued justification and new groups could not invoke rights once denied. This Court has rejected that approach, both with respect to the right to marry and the rights of gays and lesbians." (It is worth noting that Alito dissented in *Obergefell* on the basis of *Glucksberg*, and Justice Scalia dissented on the basis of *Glucksberg* in *Lawrence*).

This dispute between liberal and conservative Justices over how to understand the nature of liberty goes back even further to the debate between Justices Scalia and Brennan in Michael H. v. Gerald D., 491 U.S. 110 (1989), over how narrowly or broadly to read the nation's traditions. For the most part, the *Glucksberg* approach has been ignored except when the conservative Justices have had a majority to limit expansion of implied fundamental rights. But since the Court now has a 6-3 conservative majority, *Glucksberg* (or at least Alito's redacted version of it) is back with a vengeance.

2. *The uses of history.* Justice Alito seeks to show that the right to abortion is not deeply rooted in the nation's history and traditions. But Justice Alito has to reckon with the fact that at the Founding and in the early republic the law did not prohibit contraception nor did it ban all abortions. At common law, before quickening (roughly 16 to 20 weeks into a pregnancy), it was not a crime to abort a fetus. Alito discusses Hale and Blackstone's view that one could be prosecuted if an abortion resulted in a woman's death. But the purpose of this doctrine seems to be protecting the life of pregnant women rather than protecting unborn life prior to quickening, for if the woman was not harmed, there was no crime at common law.

Alito's stronger argument is that from the Civil War era onwards, there was a successful campaign to criminalize abortion. States began to prohibit the practice throughout pregnancy, to increase criminal sanctions, and to criminalize the use and circulation of contraceptives and abortifacients. But there are problems in tying the meaning of the Constitution's liberty guarantee to these laws if we look at the background conditions in which this campaign to restrict abortion was conducted (for example, the fact that women could neither vote nor hold office) and the kinds of arguments people advanced for banning abortion.

The larger problem with Alito's argument — and indeed, the entire *Glucksberg* approach — concerns why we think that tradition has normative authority. In general, we follow tradition because it reflects the accumulated wisdom of previous generations, so it is presumptively morally good, or at least morally acceptable. But if a tradition reflects something we think very unjust or inhumane, it loses its moral authority to guide us. For example, if a tradition arose to protect slavery or Jim Crow, one cannot use the mere fact that it is a tradition to justify it.

The problem is that the history that Alito recounts — going back to the thirteenth century — is deeply connected to the subordinate status of women, and to laws and practices that kept women subservient and denied them equal opportunities. Abortion laws were among many others that regulated women's sexuality and autonomy, and the authors Alito quotes reflect the assumptions of their day. Therefore it is not clear why the *Glucksberg* test should have any legitimacy with respect to women's sexual freedom, since it grounds the test for constitutional liberty in deeply unjust and inequitable practices. Put another way, a reason why women's reproductive rights likely would *not* be deeply rooted in the Nation's traditions is that traditionally the country was committed to keeping women from having very many rights. Conversely, it is no accident that reproductive justice claims start to get taken seriously as soon as women start to win a broad range of equal rights in American society. Indeed, abortion and contraceptive rights were key demands of the women's movement in the 1970s.

3. *Originalism and Tradition. Dobbs* is another example of how the conservative Justices' use of originalism and tradition have tended to merge in practice. (See also the discussion notes following *Bruen*). From one perspective, *Dobbs* is not, strictly speaking, an originalist opinion. It does not decide whether abortion is constitutionally protected by looking to the original meaning of the Due Process Clause in 1791 (5th Amendment) or 1868 (14th Amendment). Rather, it appears to be a *doctrinal* opinion that purports to apply the Court's doctrine of implied fundamental rights in *Glucksberg*, and it looks to history and tradition to discover what those rights are. It also accepts the doctrine of substantive due process, which many conservative originalists reject. Justice Thomas, for example, makes clear that in his view, the whole doctrine of substantive due process is inconsistent with originalism.

At the same time, Alito emphasizes that there was no right to abortion in 1868 when the Fourteenth Amendment was adopted, which looks like an argument from original expected applications or original understanding. Justice Kavanaugh asserts that what is most important to him is that abortion was mostly criminalized in 1868 and remained so until the 1970s.

Dobbs, like *Bruen*, suggests that the Court's self-described originalist judges are not strongly distinguishing originalism from traditionalism. Conservative originalists like Justice Scalia have long championed something like Alito's interpretation of *Glucksberg*, and several of the Court's end-of-term decisions — joined or written by its originalist Justices — have invoked the idea of "history and tradition."

4. *"Generalized assertions about the national psyche."* Justice Alito argues that stare decisis should not require the Court to keep *Casey*, because, among other reasons, there has been no reliance on the right to abortion in the United States.

When it upheld *Roe* on stare decisis grounds, the *Casey* Court declared that "To eliminate the issue of reliance. . . . would be simply to refuse to face the fact that, for two decades of economic and social developments, people have organized intimate relationships and made choices that define their views of themselves and their places in society, in reliance on the availability of abortion in the event that contraception should fail. The ability of women to participate equally in the economic and social life of the Nation has been facilitated by their ability to control their reproductive lives."

Alito disagrees. The kind of reliance that matters, he argues, is "very concrete reliance interests, like those that develop in 'cases involving property and contract rights.' " By contrast, women's expectation in organizing their lives that they will be able to obtain abortions if contraception fails and they become pregnant is simply too diffuse and abstract. Alito describes *Casey*'s account of women's reliance as no more than "generalized assertions about the national psyche"—not the kind of concrete reliance that the Court has concerned itself with.

Do you agree with Alito's characterization of the interests at stake? Why isn't women's ability to plan their economic, social, and family lives a very important form of reliance?

5. *Eliminating fundamental rights.* The Supreme Court has, in the past, eliminated constitutional protection for rights, for example, when it removed special protection from freedom of contract in West Coast Hotel v. Parrish. It has greatly limited the effect of the Contracts Clause from early nineteenth-century decisions. It has watered down the procedural guarantees of the Due Process Clause from where they stood in the early 1970s. Over the past fifty years the Court has significantly cut back on criminal procedure protections and eliminated much of the Establishment Clause's guarantees. But in *Dobbs* the Court removes constitutional protection from a right which it had previously declared important to women's equal participation in the "economic and social life of the Nation." Is this different in kind?

6. *Neutrality.* Justice Kavanaugh argues that the Constitution says nothing about abortion one way or the other, and that it is neutral on the subject, so the question should be left to the political process. (Compare Justice Scalia's argument in *Romer v. Evans* that the Court should stay out of cultural disputes.)

What does neutrality mean in this context? What is the baseline by which we determine whether the Constitution is neutral? If the Constitution is neutral on abortion, why should it not also be neutral on women's civil equality, the right to marry, the right to travel, the right to use contraceptives, the right to refuse medical treatment, or, indeed, the individual right to carry firearms outside the home for personal self-defense? Each of these results required the Court to interpret the Constitution's text in a controversial way. Is Kavanaugh's neutrality claim just another way of saying that he believes there is no constitutional right to abortion?

7. *Abortion rights and the rational basis test.* In his dissenting opinion in *Roe*, then-Justice Rehnquist argued that there was no fundamental right to abortion and that the appropriate test for abortion regulation was the test that applied generally to social and economic legislation—the rational basis test of Williamson

v. Lee Optical Co., 348 U.S. 483 (1955). However, Rehnquist explained, "[t]he Due Process Clause of the Fourteenth Amendment undoubtedly does place a limit, albeit a broad one, on legislative power to enact laws such as this. If the Texas statute were to prohibit an abortion even where the mother's life is in jeopardy, I have little doubt that such a statute would lack a rational relation to a valid state objective under the test stated in *Williamson*, supra."

Do you believe that the current Court would agree with Rehnquist? If the Court considered a challenge to such an abortion law, which result—upholding the law or striking it down as lacking a rational basis—would be "neutral" in Justice Kavanaugh's sense of the word?

8. *Does the Constitution forbid abortion?* In *Roe* itself, the Court considered and rejected the idea that the Due Process and Equal Protection Clauses protected unborn life as "persons." Some commentators, however, have argued that the next step after overturning *Roe* and *Casey* is to hold that fertilized ova, blastocysts, and fetuses are "persons" from the moment of conception and therefore that it is unconstitutional to allow abortion to remain legal while criminalizing murder. Joshua J. Craddock, Protecting Prenatal Persons: Does The Fourteenth Amendment Prohibit Abortion? 40 Harv. J. L. & Pub. Pol. 539 (2017); John Finnis, Abortion Is Unconstitutional, First Things, April 2021, at https://www .firstthings.com/article/2021/04/abortion-is-unconstitutional.

None of the Justices endorsed this theory, and Justice Kavanagh's concurrence— which provided the necessary fifth vote to overturn *Roe* and *Casey*—rejected the claim. Given the distance that doctrine has already travelled in a very short pace of time, one should not discount the possibility that one or more Justices may someday find the argument attractive. What consequences would this argument have for women's reproductive lives? Is this argument itself a form of substantive due process? (Consider, for example, a constitutional challenge to a federal statute protecting abortion rights).

9. *The right to travel to obtain an abortion.* Justice Kavanaugh's concurrence also asserts that states where abortion is criminalized may not prevent their citizens from traveling to other states to obtain abortions. The basis of this claim is the right to travel, also (ironically) an implied fundamental right. It was originally implied from the structure of the Union, see Crandall v. State of Nevada, 73 U.S. 35 (1867), then located in the Equal Protection Clause, see Shapiro v. Thompson, 394 U.S. 618 (1969), and is now protected by the Privileges or Immunities Clause of the Fourteenth Amendment. See Saenz v. Roe, 526 U.S. 489 (1999).

Most of the recent cases concerning the right to travel have concerned states attempting to keep new residents out, for example, by denying them welfare benefits, see *Shapiro*, supra; cf. Doe v. Bolton, 410 U.S., at 200 (1973)(under the Privileges and Immunities Clause of Article IV, section 2, States cannot limit access to abortion to their own residents). The issue post-*Dobbs* is whether states can keep their citizens from temporarily traveling to other states to obtain abortions illegal in their home state, and then returning. Cf. United States v. Guest,

383 U.S. 745, 757-759 (1966)(noting Congress's power to protect the constitutional right to move from state to state to engage in interstate commerce).

In Bigelow v. Virginia, 421 U.S. 809 (1975), a Virginia newspaper published an advertisement for abortion services in New York, where abortion was legal (when the case arose, abortion was illegal in Virginia.) The Court held that the First Amendment prevented Virginia from prohibiting the advertisement, and that Virginia could not prevent its citizens from obtaining abortions in New York:

> [T]he placement services advertised in appellant's newspaper were legally provided in New York at that time. The Virginia Legislature could not have regulated the advertiser's activity in New York, and obviously could not have proscribed the activity in that State. Neither could Virginia prevent its residents from traveling to New York to obtain those services or, as the State conceded prosecute them for going there. Virginia possessed no authority to regulate the services provided in New York — the skills and credentials of the New York physicians and of the New York professionals who assisted them, the standards of the New York hospitals and clinics to which patients were referred, or the practices and charges of the New York referral services.
>
> A State does not acquire power or supervision over the internal affairs of another State merely because the welfare and health of its own citizens may be affected when they travel to that State. It may seek to disseminate information so as to enable its citizens to make better informed decisions when they leave. But it may not, under the guise of exercising internal police powers, bar a citizen of another State from disseminating information about an activity that is legal in that State.

Along the same lines, states that prohibit gambling may not prevent their citizens from traveling to Nevada where gambling is legal and returning with their winnings. Of course, *Bigelow* was decided fifty years ago by essentially the same Court that decided *Roe*. One should not assume that the law will remain fixed. States where abortion is criminalized may try to chip away at *Bigelow* or find other devices to discourage their citizens from obtaining abortions, leading to further litigation.

For example, suppose that Missouri declares that life — and hence Missouri citizenship — begin at conception. Suppose that state officials learn that a pregnant woman living in St. Louis plans to cross the border into Illinois to obtain an abortion, which will end the life of one of its citizens. Could Missouri argue that *Bigelow* does not apply because it has a right to prevent the death of a citizen who is taken across state lines without his or her consent? Could Missouri constitutionally treat travel by pregnant women outside the state as a form of kidnapping?

10. *The fate of other implied fundamental rights after Dobbs.* In *Dobbs*, Justice Alito adopts the standard for determining the scope of protected liberties advocated by the dissenting Justices in *Lawrence* and *Obergefell*. At the same time, he goes out of his way to insist that nothing in his opinion endangers the Court's other decisions protecting gay rights, the right to marriage (including same-sex marriage) or the right of married and single persons to purchase and

use contraceptives. The reason, he explains, is that only in the case of abortion is there destruction of unborn life. "None of the other decisions cited by *Roe* and *Casey* involved the critical moral question posed by abortion. They are therefore inapposite. They do not support the right to obtain an abortion, and by the same token, our conclusion that the Constitution does not confer such a right does not undermine them in any way."

The issue is somewhat more complicated than Alito lets on, however, for three reasons.

First, Alito's argument for why *Roe* and *Casey* were clearly incorrect is *Glucksberg*'s test of whether a right is deeply rooted in our Nation's history and traditions. But rights to contraception (by married or single persons), gay rights, and the right to same-sex marriage also fail this test. (In his dissent in *Obergefell*, Alito makes clear that he believes that "it is beyond dispute that the right to same-sex marriage is not among those rights [deeply rooted in our Nation's history and traditions].").

In *Dobbs*, Alito distinguishes these cases from abortion on a different ground: none of these rights creates the same kind of harm as abortion — the destruction of a fetus. Therefore a great deal depends on whether what really matters to the Court in the long run is whether a right is deeply rooted in our Nation's history and traditions (*Glucksberg*) or whether one must also show that the exercise of the right also causes a distinctive kind of harm. Note, however, that if harm is the concern, some abortion opponents argue that some forms of contraception — for example, Plan B emergency contraception — may prevent a fertilized ovum from attaching to the uterus, guaranteeing its eventual destruction. In addition, opponents of same-sex marriage argue that it does cause deep societal harm.

Second, some of the Justices may change their minds about whether to keep these precedents. Equally important, the Court's composition may change. In 2016 the Court vigorously reaffirmed *Roe* and *Casey* in Whole Woman's Health v. Hellerstedt, 579 U.S. 582 (2016). Six years later, *Dobbs* overturned both. So a lot can happen to Supreme Court doctrine in a very short time if new Justices have different views and priorities than older ones did. And, not to put too fine a point on it, Justice Thomas has already made clear that he is ready to overturn all of the precedents Alito says are untouched by *Dobbs*.

Third, there are many ways to cut back on contraceptive rights, gay rights, and same-sex marriage without overturning existing decisions. The Justices may read these decisions narrowly or refuse to extend them in later cases. They may use the Free Speech and Free Exercise Clauses to limit their impact. Thus, one should not assume that *Dobbs* is the furthest the Court will go in cutting back on implied fundamental rights any more than one should assume that *Bruen* is the furthest the Court will go in protecting Second Amendment rights.

11. *The coming battles over reproductive rights.* Overturning *Roe* and *Casey* will not put an end to constitutional litigation over abortion rights. States with pro-life legislatures will likely pass a series of laws designed to keep their citizens from obtaining abortions by traveling out of state or obtaining abortion medication.

States may also attempt to deter people from assisting others in obtaining abortions. For example, while the Court was considering *Dobbs*, Texas passed S.B. 8, the Heartbeat Act, which outlawed abortions once a fetal heartbeat is detectable (usually around the sixth week of pregnancy). S.B. 8 prohibits state officials from enforcing the statute but allows any citizen to sue any other person for performing an abortion or assisting another in the performance of an abortion, and if successful, to obtain an injunction and recoup a minimum of 10,000 dollars in damages. The Supreme Court refused to prevent the enforcement of this law, leading many to suspect that it would soon overturn *Roe* and *Casey*. Whole Woman's Health v. Jackson, 142 S. Ct. 522 (2021).

The status of IUD's and emergency contraception also remains unclear following *Dobbs*, because some states may assert that they act as abortifacients. States that protect life from the moment of conception may also try to regulate in vitro fertilization, because it creates more embryos than can be implanted in a woman and the question remains how and whether doctors may dispose of them. States may turn to electronic surveillance to identify whether women are pregnant and considering abortions and seek to prevent them or punish those who assist them.

Conversely, if the federal government attempts to protect abortion rights by statute, this will produce a series of constitutional challenges. Abortion opponents may challenge a federal abortion law under the Court's Commerce Clause and Spending Clause precedents. Abortion opponents may argue that if federal law simply forbids states from passing laws banning abortion this would violate the anti-commandeering principle of New York v. United States and Murphy v. NCAA. If a federal law attempts to preempt state abortion legislation, there will be litigation about what kinds of state laws are actually preempted. Finally, because *Dobbs* says there is no underlying constitutional right to abortion, basing the statute on Congress's Section 5 powers to enforce the Fourteenth Amendment may lead to a challenge under City of Boerne v. Flores.

These examples merely scratch the surface of the constitutional questions that may arise in the future. Justice Kavanaugh's hope that the Court could simply maintain a position of neutrality and send abortion issues back to the states and Congress will probably prove as unrealistic as the *Casey*'s plurality's hope that its compromise could help resolve differences over abortion.

12. *The future of equality arguments for reproductive rights.* Justice Alito devotes only a single paragraph to rejecting equality arguments for abortion, hoping preemptively to settle the question once and for all. He treats the issue as "squarely foreclosed by our precedents." But as with several other features of his opinion, the issue is more complicated than Alito lets on. Equality remains an emerging ground for the protection of abortion rights, not only in the federal courts, but especially in the states.

Equality may also play a role not only in federal legislation but also in litigation. *Geduldig* and *Bray*, which Alito relies on to reject equality arguments, have been limited by two later cases, *Hibbs* and United States v. Virginia (see the discussion in Chapter Eight). In *Dobbs* the dissenters did not directly reply to Alito's arguments, probably because the case was litigated in terms of due process, and not equal protection. Instead the dissenters echoed language in *Casey* about abortion being necessary to women's equal citizenship status. They emphasized "women's opportunities to participate fully and equally in the Nation's political, social, and economic life," and continuously invoked liberty and equality together as the basis of the abortion right. Given the majority's perfunctory discussion of equality in *Dobbs*, a later court may regard the question of how the Equal Protection Clause applies as still open. Certainly state courts interpreting their own constitutions may choose to follow the later cases, *Hibbs* and *Virginia*. And as we have seen in other contexts (for example, the movement for marriage equality), victories in the state courts often are necessary before a claim gets taken seriously in the federal courts.

Second, *Glucksberg*'s test of history and tradition applies only to the Due Process Clause. It does not apply to the Court's equal protection jurisprudence, and for an obvious reason: When people have argued for expanding equal rights and equal citizenship, they have usually been *criticizing* long standing social arrangements and status hierarchies rather than appealing to them. So the fact that there is a long tradition of treating people unequally is generally not a winning argument in equal protection law. Quite the contrary, it is often a justification for recognizing equal rights.

Insert at the end of p. 1740:

NEW YORK STATE RIFLE & PISTOL ASSOCIATION, INC. v. BRUEN
142 S.Ct. 2111 (2022)

[The State of New York makes it a crime to possess a firearm without a license, whether inside or outside the home. An individual who wants to carry a firearm outside his home may obtain an unrestricted license to "have and carry" a concealed "pistol or revolver" if he can prove that "proper cause exists" for doing so. N. Y. Penal Law Ann. § 400.00(2)(f). An applicant satisfies the "proper cause" requirement only if he can "demonstrate a special need for self-protection distinguishable from that of the general community." The licensing regulation dates back over a century to 1911.

Petitioners Brandon Koch and Robert Nash are law-abiding, adult citizens of Rensselaer County, New York. Both are members of Petitioner New York State Rifle & Pistol Association, Inc., a public-interest group organized to defend the Second Amendment rights of New Yorkers. New York granted Nash and Koch a restricted license for hunting and target shooting only. Both applied for a general unrestricted license: Nash alleged that there were a series of recent robberies in his neighborhood, and Koch cited his extensive experience in safely handling firearms. The state refused both requests, but Koch was permitted to carry a firearm to and from work. All three petitioners sued, arguing that *Heller* and *McDonald* protected the right to carry firearms outside the home for self-defense without any special showing of need.]

Justice THOMAS delivered the opinion of the Court.

[I]n 43 States, the government issues licenses to carry based on objective criteria. But in six States, including New York, the government further conditions issuance of a license to carry on a citizen's showing of some additional special need. Because the State of New York issues public-carry licenses only when an applicant demonstrates a special need for self-defense, we conclude that the State's licensing regime violates the Constitution. . . .

I

A

When a licensing officer denies an application, judicial review is limited. New York courts defer to an officer's application of the proper-cause standard unless it is "arbitrary and capricious." In other words, the decision "must be upheld if the record shows a rational basis for it." The rule leaves applicants little recourse if their local licensing officer denies a permit.

New York is not alone in requiring a permit to carry a handgun in public. But the vast majority of States — 43 by our count — are "shall issue" jurisdictions, where authorities must issue concealed-carry licenses whenever applicants satisfy certain threshold requirements, without granting licensing officials discretion to deny licenses based on a perceived lack of need or suitability. Meanwhile, only six States and the District of Columbia have "may issue" licensing laws, under which authorities have discretion to deny concealed-carry licenses even when the applicant satisfies the statutory criteria, usually because the applicant has not demonstrated cause or suitability for the relevant license. Aside from New York, then, only California, the District of Columbia, Hawaii, Maryland, Massachusetts, and New Jersey have analogues to the "proper cause" standard.[2] All of these "proper cause" analogues have been upheld by the Courts of Appeals, save for the District of Columbia's, which has been permanently enjoined since 2017. . . .

II

[I]n keeping with *Heller*, we hold that when the Second Amendment's plain text covers an individual's conduct, the Constitution presumptively protects that conduct. To justify its regulation, the government may not simply posit that the regulation promotes an important interest. Rather, the government must demonstrate that the regulation is consistent with this Nation's historical tradition of firearm regulation. Only if a firearm regulation is consistent with this Nation's historical tradition may a court conclude that the individual's conduct falls outside the Second Amendment's "unqualified command."

A

Since *Heller* and *McDonald*, the two-step test that Courts of Appeals have developed to assess Second Amendment claims proceeds as follows. At the first step, the government may justify its regulation by "establish[ing] that the challenged law regulates activity falling outside the scope of the right as originally understood." The Courts of Appeals then ascertain the original scope of the right based on its historical meaning. But if the historical evidence at this step is "inconclusive or suggests that the regulated activity is *not* categorically unprotected," the courts generally proceed to step two.

At the second step, courts often analyze "how close the law comes to the core of the Second Amendment right and the severity of the law's burden on that right." The Courts of Appeals generally maintain "that the core Second Amendment right is limited to self-defense *in the home*." If a "core" Second Amendment right is burdened, courts apply "strict scrutiny" and ask whether the Government can prove that the law is "narrowly tailored to achieve a compelling governmental interest." Otherwise, they apply intermediate scrutiny and consider whether the Government can show that the regulation is "substantially related to the achievement of an important governmental interest." Both respondents and the United States largely agree with this consensus, arguing that intermediate scrutiny is appropriate when text and history are unclear in attempting to delineate the scope of the right.

B

Despite the popularity of this two-step approach, it is one step too many. Step one of the predominant framework is broadly consistent with *Heller*, which demands a test rooted in the Second Amendment's text, as informed by history. But *Heller* and *McDonald* do not support applying means-end scrutiny in the Second Amendment context. Instead, the government must affirmatively prove that its firearms regulation is part of the historical tradition that delimits the outer bounds of the right to keep and bear arms. . . .

[W]hether it came to defining the character of the right (individual or militia dependent), suggesting the outer limits of the right, or assessing the constitutionality of a particular regulation, *Heller* relied on text and history. It did not invoke any means-end test such as strict or intermediate scrutiny.

Moreover, *Heller* and *McDonald* expressly rejected the application of any "judge-empowering 'interest-balancing inquiry' that 'asks whether the statute burdens a protected interest in a way or to an extent that is out of proportion to the statute's salutary effects upon other important governmental interests.'" *Heller*, 554 U.S. at 634; see also *McDonald*, 561 U.S. at 790-791, 130 S.Ct. 3020 (plurality opinion) (the Second Amendment does not permit—let alone require—"judges to assess the costs and benefits of firearms restrictions" under means-end scrutiny). We declined to engage in means-end scrutiny because "[t]he very enumeration of the right takes out of the hands of government—even the Third Branch of Government—the power to decide on a case-by-case basis whether the right is *really worth* insisting upon." *Heller*. We then concluded: "A constitutional guarantee subject to future judges' assessments of its usefulness is no constitutional guarantee at all."

Not only did *Heller* decline to engage in means-end scrutiny generally, but it also specifically ruled out the intermediate-scrutiny test that respondents and the United States now urge us to adopt. . . . . We reiterate that the standard for applying the Second Amendment is as follows: When the Second Amendment's plain text covers an individual's conduct, the Constitution presumptively protects that conduct. The government must then justify its regulation by demonstrating that it is consistent with the Nation's historical tradition of firearm regulation. Only then may a court conclude that the individual's conduct falls outside the Second Amendment's "unqualified command."

C

This Second Amendment standard accords with how we protect other constitutional rights. Take, for instance, the freedom of speech in the First Amendment. . . . "[W]hen the Government restricts speech, the Government bears the burden of proving the constitutionality of its actions." In some cases, that burden includes showing whether the expressive conduct falls outside of the category of protected speech. And to carry that burden, the government must generally point to *historical* evidence about the reach of the First Amendment's protections. See, *e.g.*, *United States v. Stevens*, 559 U.S. 460, 468-471 (2010) (placing the burden on the government to show that a type of speech belongs to a "historic and traditional categor[y]" of constitutionally unprotected speech "long familiar to the bar" (internal quotation marks omitted)).

And beyond the freedom of speech, our focus on history also comports with how we assess many other constitutional claims. If a litigant asserts the right in court to "be confronted with the witnesses against him," U.S. Const., Amdt. 6, we require courts to consult history to determine the scope of that right. See, *e.g.*, *Giles v. California*, 554 U.S. 353, 358 (2008) ("admitting only those exceptions [to the Confrontation Clause] established at the time of the founding" (internal quotation marks omitted)). Similarly, when a litigant claims a violation of his rights under the Establishment Clause, Members of this Court "loo[k] to history for guidance." *American Legion v. American Humanist Assn.*, 588 U.S. ——, ——, 139 S.Ct. 2067, 2087, 204 L.Ed.2d 452 (2019) (plurality opinion). We adopt a similar approach here.

To be sure, "[h]istorical analysis can be difficult; it sometimes requires resolving threshold questions, and making nuanced judgments about which evidence to consult and how to interpret it." But reliance on history to inform the meaning of constitutional text—especially text meant to codify a *pre-existing* right—is, in our view, more legitimate, and more administrable, than asking judges to "make difficult empirical judgments" about "the costs and benefits of firearms restrictions," especially given their "lack [of] expertise" in the field.

The dissent claims that *Heller*'s text-and-history test will prove unworkable compared to means-end scrutiny in part because judges are relatively ill equipped to "resolv[e] difficult historical questions" or engage in "searching historical surveys." We are unpersuaded. The job of judges is not to resolve historical questions in the abstract; it is to resolve *legal* questions presented in particular cases or controversies. That "legal inquiry is a refined subset" of a broader "historical inquiry," and it relies on "various evidentiary principles and default rules" to resolve uncertainties. W. Baude & S. Sachs, Originalism and the Law of the Past, 37 L. & Hist. Rev. 809, 810-811 (2019). For example, "[i]n our adversarial system of adjudication, we follow the principle of party presentation." *United States v. Sineneng-Smith*, 590 U.S. ——, ——, 140 S.Ct. 1575, 1579. Courts are thus entitled to decide a case based on the historical record compiled by the parties. [relocated footnote—eds.]

If the last decade of Second Amendment litigation has taught this Court anything, it is that federal courts tasked with making such difficult empirical judgments regarding firearm regulations under the banner of "intermediate scrutiny" often defer to the determinations of legislatures. But while that judicial deference to legislative interest balancing is understandable—and, elsewhere, appropriate—it is not deference that the Constitution demands here. The Second Amendment "is the very *product* of an interest balancing by the people" and it "surely elevates above all other interests the right of law-abiding, responsible citizens to use arms" for self-defense. *Heller*. It is this balance—struck by the traditions of the American people—that demands our unqualified deference.

D

The test that we set forth in *Heller* and apply today requires courts to assess whether modern firearms regulations are consistent with the Second Amendment's text and historical understanding. In some cases, that inquiry will be fairly straightforward. For instance, when a challenged regulation addresses a general societal problem that has persisted since the 18th century, the lack of a distinctly similar historical regulation addressing that problem is relevant evidence that the challenged regulation is inconsistent with the Second Amendment. Likewise, if earlier generations addressed the societal problem, but did so through materially different means, that also could be evidence that a modern regulation is unconstitutional. And if some jurisdictions actually attempted to enact analogous regulations during this timeframe, but those proposals were rejected on constitutional grounds, that rejection surely would provide some probative evidence of unconstitutionality.

Heller itself exemplifies this kind of straightforward historical inquiry. One of the District's regulations challenged in *Heller* "totally ban[ned] handgun possession in the home." The District in *Heller* addressed a perceived societal problem—firearm violence in densely populated communities—and it employed a regulation—a flat ban on the possession of handguns in the home—that the Founders themselves could have adopted to confront that problem. Accordingly, after considering "founding-era historical precedent," including "various restrictive laws in the colonial period," and finding that none was analogous to the District's ban, *Heller* concluded that the handgun ban was unconstitutional.

New York's proper-cause requirement concerns the same alleged societal problem addressed in *Heller*: "handgun violence," primarily in "urban area[s]." Following the course charted by *Heller*, we will consider whether "historical precedent" from before, during, and even after the founding evinces a comparable tradition of regulation. And, as we explain below, we find no such tradition in the historical materials that respondents and their *amici* have brought to bear on that question.

While the historical analogies here and in *Heller* are relatively simple to draw, other cases implicating unprecedented societal concerns or dramatic technological changes may require a more nuanced approach. The regulatory challenges posed by firearms today are not always the same as those that preoccupied the Founders in 1791 or the Reconstruction generation in 1868. Fortunately, the Founders created a Constitution—and a Second Amendment—"intended to endure for ages to come, and consequently, to be adapted to the various crises of human affairs." *McCulloch v. Maryland*. Although its meaning is fixed according to the understandings of those who ratified it, the Constitution can, and must, apply to circumstances beyond those the Founders specifically anticipated. . . .

We have already recognized in *Heller* at least one way in which the Second Amendment's historically fixed meaning applies to new circumstances: Its reference to "arms" does not apply "only [to] those arms in existence in the 18th century." "Just as the First Amendment protects modern forms of communications, and the Fourth Amendment applies to modern forms of search, the Second Amendment extends, prima facie, to all instruments that constitute bearable arms, even those that were not in existence at the time of the founding." Thus, even though the Second Amendment's definition of "arms" is fixed according to its historical understanding, that general definition covers modern instruments that facilitate armed self-defense. Cf. *Caetano v. Massachusetts*, 577 U.S. 411, 411-412 (2016) (*per curiam*) (stun guns).

Much like we use history to determine which modern "arms" are protected by the Second Amendment, so too does history guide our consideration of modern regulations that were unimaginable at the founding. When confronting such present-day firearm regulations, this historical inquiry that courts must conduct will often involve reasoning by analogy—a commonplace task for any lawyer or judge. Like all analogical reasoning, determining whether a historical regulation is a proper analogue for a distinctly modern firearm regulation requires a determination of whether the two regulations are "relevantly similar." And because "[e]verything is similar in infinite ways to everything else," one needs "some metric enabling the analogizer to assess which similarities are important and which are not," For instance, a green truck and a green hat are relevantly similar if one's metric is "things that are green." They are not relevantly similar if the applicable metric is "things you can wear."

While we do not now provide an exhaustive survey of the features that render regulations relevantly similar under the Second Amendment, we do think that *Heller* and *McDonald* point toward at least two metrics: how and why the regulations burden a law-abiding citizen's right to armed self-defense. As we stated in *Heller* and repeated in *McDonald*, "individual self-defense is 'the *central component*' of the Second Amendment right." Therefore, whether modern and historical regulations impose a comparable burden on the right of armed self-defense and whether that burden is comparably justified are " '*central*' " considerations when engaging in an analogical inquiry.

This does not mean that courts may engage in independent means-end scrutiny under the guise of an analogical inquiry. Again, the Second Amendment is the "product of an interest balancing *by the people*," not the evolving product of federal judges. Analogical reasoning requires judges to apply faithfully the balance struck by the founding generation to modern circumstances, and contrary to the dissent's assertion, there is nothing "[i]roni[c]" about that undertaking. It is not an invitation to revise that balance through means-end scrutiny. [relocated footnote—eds.]

To be clear, analogical reasoning under the Second Amendment is neither a regulatory straightjacket nor a regulatory blank check. On the one hand, courts should not "uphold every modern law that remotely resembles a historical analogue," because doing so "risk[s] endorsing outliers that our ancestors would never have accepted." On the other hand, analogical reasoning requires only that the government identify a well-established and representative historical *analogue*, not a historical *twin*. So even if a modern-day regulation is not a dead ringer for historical precursors, it still may be analogous enough to pass constitutional muster.

Consider, for example, *Heller*'s discussion of "longstanding" "laws forbidding the carrying of firearms in sensitive places such as schools and government buildings." Although the historical record yields relatively few 18th- and 19th-century "sensitive places" where weapons were altogether prohibited—*e.g.,* legislative assemblies, polling places, and courthouses—we are also aware of no disputes regarding the lawfulness of such prohibitions. We therefore can assume it settled that these locations were "sensitive places" where arms carrying could be prohibited consistent with the Second Amendment. And courts can use analogies to those historical regulations of "sensitive places" to determine that modern regulations prohibiting the carry of firearms in *new* and analogous sensitive places are constitutionally permissible.

Although we have no occasion to comprehensively define "sensitive places" in this case, we do think respondents err in their attempt to characterize New York's proper-cause requirement as a "sensitive-place" law. In their view, "sensitive places" where the government may lawfully disarm law-abiding citizens include all "places where people typically congregate and where law-enforcement and other public-safety professionals are presumptively available." It is true that people sometimes congregate in "sensitive places," and it is likewise true that law enforcement professionals are usually presumptively available in those locations. But expanding the category of "sensitive places" simply to all places of public congregation that are not isolated from law enforcement defines the category of "sensitive places" far too broadly. Respondents' argument would in effect exempt cities from the Second Amendment and would eviscerate the general right to publicly carry arms for self-defense that we discuss in detail below. Put simply, there is no historical basis for New York to effectively declare the island of Manhattan a "sensitive place" simply because it is crowded and protected generally by the New York City Police Department.

Like *Heller*, we "do not undertake an exhaustive historical analysis . . . of the full scope of the Second Amendment." And we acknowledge that "applying constitutional principles to novel modern conditions can be difficult and leave close questions at the margins." "But that is hardly unique to the Second Amendment. It is an essential component of judicial decisionmaking under our enduring Constitution." We see no reason why judges frequently tasked with answering these kinds of historical, analogical questions cannot do the same for Second Amendment claims.

III

Having made the constitutional standard endorsed in *Heller* more explicit, we now apply that standard to New York's proper-cause requirement.

A

It is undisputed that petitioners Koch and Nash—two ordinary, law-abiding, adult citizens—are part of "the people" whom the Second Amendment protects. Nor does any party dispute that handguns are weapons "in common use" today for self-defense. We therefore turn to whether the plain text of the Second Amendment protects Koch's and Nash's proposed course of conduct—carrying handguns publicly for self-defense.

We have little difficulty concluding that it does. Respondents do not dispute this. Nor could they. Nothing in the Second Amendment's text draws a home/public distinction with respect to the right to keep and bear arms. As we explained in *Heller*, the "textual elements" of the Second Amendment's operative clause—"the right of the people to keep and bear Arms, shall not be infringed"—"guarantee the individual right to possess and carry weapons in case of confrontation." *Heller* further confirmed that the right to "bear arms" refers to the right to "wear, bear, or carry . . . upon the person or in the clothing or in a pocket, for the purpose . . . of being armed and ready for offensive or defensive action in a case of conflict with another person."

This definition of "bear" naturally encompasses public carry. Most gun owners do not wear a holstered pistol at their hip in their bedroom or while sitting at the dinner table. Although individuals often "keep" firearms in their home, at the ready for self-defense, most do not "bear" (*i.e.*, carry) them in the home beyond moments of actual confrontation. To confine the right to "bear" arms to the home would nullify half of the Second Amendment's operative protections.

Moreover, confining the right to "bear" arms to the home would make little sense given that self-defense is "the *central component* of the [Second Amendment] right itself." After all, the Second Amendment guarantees an "individual right to possess and carry weapons in case of confrontation," and confrontation can surely take place outside the home.

Although we remarked in *Heller* that the need for armed self-defense is perhaps "most acute" in the home, we did not suggest that the need was insignificant elsewhere. Many Americans hazard greater danger outside the home than in it. The text of the Second Amendment reflects that reality. . . .

B

[T]he burden [then] falls on respondents to show that New York's proper-cause requirement is consistent with this Nation's historical tradition of firearm regulation. . . .

Respondents appeal to a variety of historical sources from the late 1200s to the early 1900s. We categorize these periods as follows: (1) medieval to early modern England; (2) the American Colonies and the early Republic; (3) antebellum America; (4) Reconstruction; and (5) the late-19th and early-20th centuries.

We categorize these historical sources because, when it comes to interpreting the Constitution, not all history is created equal. "Constitutional rights are enshrined with the scope they were understood to have *when the people adopted them.*" *Heller*. The Second Amendment was adopted in 1791; the Fourteenth in 1868. Historical evidence that long predates either date may not illuminate the scope of the right if linguistic or legal conventions changed in the intervening years. It is one thing for courts to "reac[h] back to the 14th century" for English practices that "prevailed up to the 'period immediately before and after the framing of the Constitution.' ". It is quite another to rely on an "ancient" practice that had become "obsolete in England at the time of the adoption of the Constitution" and never "was acted upon or accepted in the colonies."

As with historical evidence generally, courts must be careful when assessing evidence concerning English common-law rights. The common law, of course, developed over time. And English common-law practices and understandings at any given time in history cannot be indiscriminately attributed to the Framers of our own Constitution. Even "the words of *Magna Charta*"—foundational as they were to the rights of America's forefathers—"stood for very different things at the time of the separation of the American Colonies from what they represented originally" in 1215. Sometimes, in interpreting our own Constitution, "it [is] better not to go too far back into antiquity for the best securities of our liberties," unless evidence shows that medieval law survived to become our Founders' law. A long, unbroken line of common-law precedent stretching from Bracton to Blackstone is far more likely to be part of our law than a short-lived, 14th-century English practice.

Similarly, we must also guard against giving postenactment history more weight than it can rightly bear. It is true that in *Heller* we reiterated that evidence of "how the Second Amendment was interpreted from immediately after its ratification through the end of the 19th century" represented a "critical tool of constitutional interpretation." We therefore examined "a variety of legal and other sources to determine *the public understanding* of [the Second Amendment] after its . . . ratification." And, in other contexts, we have explained that " 'a regular course of practice' can 'liquidate & settle the meaning of' disputed or indeterminate 'terms & phrases' " in the Constitution. In other words, we recognize that "where a governmental practice has been open, widespread, and unchallenged since the early days of the Republic, the practice should guide our interpretation of an ambiguous constitutional provision."

But to the extent later history contradicts what the text says, the text controls. " '[L]iquidating' indeterminacies in written laws is far removed from expanding or altering them." Thus, "post-ratification adoption or acceptance of laws that are *inconsistent* with the original meaning of the constitutional text obviously cannot overcome or alter that text."

As we recognized in *Heller* itself, because post-Civil War discussions of the right to keep and bear arms "took place 75 years after the ratification of the Second Amendment, they do not provide as much insight into its original meaning as earlier sources." . . . . *Heller*'s interest in mid- to late-19th-century commentary was secondary. *Heller* considered this evidence "only after surveying what it regarded as a wealth of authority for its reading—including the text of the Second Amendment and state constitutions." In other words, this 19th-century evidence was "treated as mere confirmation of what the Court thought had already been established."

A final word on historical method: Strictly speaking, New York is bound to respect the right to keep and bear arms because of the Fourteenth Amendment, not the Second. Nonetheless, we have made clear that individual rights enumerated in the Bill of Rights and made applicable against the States through the Fourteenth Amendment have the same scope as against the Federal Government. And we have generally assumed that the scope of the protection applicable to the Federal Government and States is pegged to the public understanding of the right when the Bill of Rights was adopted in 1791.

We also acknowledge that there is an ongoing scholarly debate on whether courts should primarily rely on the prevailing understanding of an individual right when the Fourteenth Amendment was ratified in 1868 when defining its scope (as well as the scope of the right against the Federal Government). See, *e.g.*, A. Amar, The Bill of Rights: Creation and Reconstruction xiv, 223, 243 (1998); K. Lash, Re-Speaking the Bill of Rights: A New Doctrine of Incorporation (Jan. 15, 2021) (manuscript, at 2), https://papers.ssrn.com/sol3/papers.cfm?abstract_id=3766917 ("When the people adopted the Fourteenth Amendment into existence, they readopted the original Bill of Rights, and did so in a manner that invested those original 1791 texts with new 1868 meanings"). We need not address this issue today because, as we explain below, the public understanding of the right to keep and bear arms in both 1791 and 1868 was, for all relevant purposes, the same with respect to public carry.

* * *

With these principles in mind, we turn to respondents' historical evidence. Throughout modern Anglo-American history, the right to keep and bear arms in public has traditionally been subject to well-defined restrictions governing the intent for which one could carry arms, the manner of carry, or the exceptional circumstances under which one could not carry arms. But apart from a handful of late-19th-century jurisdictions, the historical record compiled by respondents does not demonstrate a tradition of broadly prohibiting the public carry of commonly used firearms for self-defense. Nor is there any such historical tradition limiting public carry only to those law-abiding citizens who demonstrate a special need for self-defense.[9] We conclude that respondents have failed to meet their burden to identify an American tradition justifying New York's proper-cause requirement. Under *Heller*'s text-and-history standard, the proper-cause requirement is therefore unconstitutional.

. . . To be clear, nothing in our analysis should be interpreted to suggest the unconstitutionality of the 43 States' "shall-issue" licensing regimes, under which "a general desire for self-defense is sufficient to obtain a [permit]." Because these licensing regimes do not require applicants to show an atypical need for armed self-defense, they do not necessarily prevent "law-abiding, responsible citizens" from exercising their Second Amendment right to public carry. Rather, it appears that these shall-issue regimes, which often require applicants to undergo a background check or pass a firearms safety course, are designed to ensure only that those bearing arms in the jurisdiction are, in fact, "law-abiding, responsible citizens." And they likewise appear to contain only "narrow, objective, and definite standards" guiding licensing officials, rather than requiring the "appraisal of facts, the exercise of judgment, and the formation of an opinion"—features that typify proper-cause standards like New York's. That said, because any permitting scheme can be put toward abusive ends, we do not rule out constitutional challenges to shall-issue regimes where, for example, lengthy wait times in processing license applications or exorbitant fees deny ordinary citizens their right to public carry. [relocated footnote—eds.]

1

Respondents' substantial reliance on English history and custom before the founding makes some sense given our statement in *Heller* that the Second Amendment "codified a right 'inherited from our English ancestors.'" But this Court has long cautioned that the English common law "is not to be taken in all respects to be that of America." Thus, "[t]he language of the Constitution cannot be interpreted safely except by reference to the common law and to British institutions *as they were when the instrument was framed and adopted,*" not as they existed in the Middle Ages.

We interpret the English history that respondents and the United States muster in light of these interpretive principles. We find that history ambiguous at best and see little reason to think that the Framers would have thought it applicable in the New World. It is not sufficiently probative to defend New York's proper-cause requirement.

To begin, respondents and their *amici* point to several medieval English regulations from as early as 1285 that they say indicate a longstanding tradition of restricting the public carry of firearms. The most prominent is the 1328 Statute of Northampton (or Statute), passed shortly after Edward II was deposed by force of arms and his son, Edward III, took the throne of a kingdom where "tendency to turmoil and rebellion was everywhere apparent throughout the realm." . . . . The Statute of Northampton was, in part, "a product of . . . the acute disorder that still plagued England." It provided that, with some exceptions, Englishmen could not "come before the King's Justices, or other of the King's Ministers doing their office, with force and arms, nor bring no force in affray of the peace, nor to go nor ride armed by night nor by day, in Fairs, Markets, nor in the presence of the Justices or other Ministers, nor in no part elsewhere, upon pain to forfeit their Armour to the King, and their Bodies to Prison at the King's pleasure."

Respondents argue that the prohibition on "rid[ing]" or "go[ing] . . . armed" was a sweeping restriction on public carry of self-defense weapons that would ultimately be adopted in Colonial America and justify onerous public-carry regulations. [But] the Statute of Northampton—at least as it was understood during the Middle Ages—has little bearing on the Second Amendment adopted in 1791. . . . The Statute's prohibition on going or riding "armed" obviously did not contemplate handguns, given they did not appear in Europe until about the mid-1500s. Rather, it appears to have been centrally concerned with the wearing of armor [or] such weapons as the "launcegay," a 10- to 12-foot-long lightweight lance. . . . Respondents point to no evidence suggesting the Statute applied to the smaller medieval weapons [such as daggers carried on the person] that strike us as most analogous to modern handguns.

When handguns were introduced in England during the Tudor and early Stuart eras, they did prompt royal efforts at suppression. . . .[because] Henry VIII worried that handguns threatened Englishmen's proficiency with the longbow—a weapon many believed was crucial to English military victories in the 1300s and 1400s, including the legendary English victories at Crécy and Agincourt. [But] by the time Englishmen began to arrive in America in the early 1600s, the public carry of handguns was no longer widely proscribed.

When we look to the latter half of the 17th century, respondents' case only weakens. As in *Heller*, we consider this history "[b]etween the [Stuart] Restoration [in 1660] and the Glorious Revolution [in 1688]" to be particularly instructive. During that time, the Stuart Kings Charles II and James II ramped up efforts to disarm their political opponents, an experience that "caused Englishmen . . . to be jealous of their arms.". . . . Parliament responded by writing the "predecessor to our Second Amendment" into the 1689 English Bill of Rights, guaranteeing that "Protestants . . . may have Arms for their Defence suitable to their Conditions, and as allowed by Law." Although this right was initially limited—it was restricted to Protestants and held only against the Crown, but not Parliament—it represented a watershed in English history. Englishmen had "never before claimed . . . the right of the individual to arms." And as that individual right matured, "by the time of the founding," the right to keep and bear arms was "understood to be an individual right protecting against both public and private violence." *Heller.*

[T]he Statute of Northampton . . . was no obstacle to public carry for self-defense in the decades leading to the founding. Serjeant William Hawkins, in his widely read 1716 treatise, confirmed that "no wearing of Arms is within the meaning of [the Statute of Northampton], unless it be accompanied with such Circumstances as are apt to terrify the People." . . . Respondents do not offer any evidence showing that, in the early 18th century or after, the mere public carrying of a handgun would terrify people. In fact, the opposite seems to have been true. As time went on, "domestic gun culture [in England] softened" any "terror" that firearms might once have conveyed. Thus, whatever place handguns had in English society during the Tudor and Stuart reigns, by the time we reach the 18th century—and near the founding—they had gained a fairly secure footing in English culture.

At the very least, we cannot conclude from this historical record that, by the time of the founding, English law would have justified restricting the right to publicly bear arms suited for self-defense only to those who demonstrate some special need for self-protection.

2

Respondents next point us to the history of the Colonies and early Republic, but there is little evidence of an early American practice of regulating public carry by the general public. . . . . In the colonial era, respondents point to only three restrictions on public carry. For starters, we doubt that *three* colonial regulations could suffice to show a tradition of public-carry regulation. In any event, even looking at these laws on their own terms, we are not convinced that they regulated public carry akin to the New York law before us. . . . Far from banning the carrying of any class of firearms, they merely codified the existing common-law offense of bearing arms to terrorize the people, as had the Statute of Northampton itself. . . .

Regardless, even if respondents' reading of these colonial statutes were correct, it would still do little to support restrictions on the public carry of handguns *today*. At most, respondents can show that colonial legislatures sometimes prohibited the carrying of "dangerous and unusual weapons"—a fact we already acknowledged in *Heller.* Drawing from this historical tradition, we explained there that the Second Amendment protects only the carrying of weapons that are those "in common use at the time," as opposed to those that "are highly unusual in society at large." Whatever the likelihood that handguns were considered "dangerous and unusual" during the colonial period, they are indisputably in "common use" for self-defense today. They are, in fact, "the quintessential self-defense weapon." Thus, even if these colonial laws prohibited the carrying of handguns because they were considered "dangerous and unusual weapons" in the 1690s, they provide no justification for laws restricting the public carry of weapons that are unquestionably in common use today. . . .

3

Only after the ratification of the Second Amendment in 1791 did public-carry restrictions proliferate. Respondents rely heavily on these restrictions, which generally fell into three categories: common-law offenses, statutory prohibitions, and "surety" statutes. None of these restrictions imposed a substantial burden on public carry analogous to the burden created by New York's restrictive licensing regime.

Common-Law Offenses. As during the colonial and founding periods, the common-law offenses of "affray" or going armed "to the terror of the people" continued to impose some limits on firearm carry in the antebellum period. But as with the earlier periods, there is no evidence indicating that these common-law limitations impaired the right of the general population to peaceable public carry. . . .

Statutory Prohibitions. In the early to mid-19th century, some States began enacting laws that proscribed the concealed carry of pistols and other small weapons. As we recognized in *Heller*, "the majority of the 19th-century courts to consider the question held that [these] prohibitions on carrying concealed weapons were lawful under the Second Amendment or state analogues." Respondents unsurprisingly cite these statutes — and decisions upholding them — as evidence that States were historically free to ban public carry.

In fact, however, the history reveals a consensus that States could *not* ban public carry altogether. Respondents' cited opinions agreed that concealed-carry prohibitions were constitutional only if they did not similarly prohibit *open* carry. . . . All told, these antebellum state-court decisions evince a consensus view that States could not altogether prohibit the public carry of "arms" protected by the Second Amendment or state analogues.

Surety Statutes. In the mid-19th century, many jurisdictions began adopting surety statutes that required certain individuals to post bond before carrying weapons in public. [But] [t]hese laws were not *bans* on public carry, and they typically targeted only those threatening to do harm. . . . Contrary to respondents' position, these "reasonable-cause laws" in no way represented the "direct precursor" to the proper-cause requirement. While New York presumes that individuals have *no* public carry right without a showing of heightened need, the surety statutes *presumed* that individuals had a right to public carry that could be burdened only if another could make out a specific showing of "reasonable cause to fear an injury, or breach of the peace." . . . Thus, unlike New York's regime, a showing of special need was required only *after* an individual was reasonably accused of intending to injure another or breach the peace. And, even then, proving special need simply avoided a fee rather than a ban. All told, therefore, "[u]nder surety laws . . . everyone started out with robust carrying rights" and only those reasonably accused were required to show a special need in order to avoid posting a bond. These antebellum special-need requirements "did not expand carrying for the responsible; it shrank burdens on carrying by the (allegedly) reckless." . . .

To summarize: The historical evidence from antebellum America does demonstrate that *the manner* of public carry was subject to reasonable regulation. Under the common law, individuals could not carry deadly weapons in a manner likely to terrorize others. Similarly, although surety statutes did not directly restrict public carry, they did provide financial incentives for responsible arms carrying. Finally, States could lawfully eliminate one kind of public carry — concealed carry — so long as they left open the option to carry openly.

None of these historical limitations on the right to bear arms approach New York's proper-cause requirement because none operated to prevent law-abiding citizens with ordinary self-defense needs from carrying arms in public for that purpose.

4

Evidence from around the adoption of the Fourteenth Amendment also fails to support respondents' position. For the most part, respondents and the United States ignore the "outpouring of discussion of the [right to keep and bear arms] in Congress and in public discourse, as people debated whether and how to secure constitutional rights for newly free slaves" after the Civil War. On July 6, 1868, Congress extended the 1866 Freedmen's Bureau Act, see 15 Stat. 83, and reaffirmed that freedmen were entitled to the "full and equal benefit of all laws and proceedings concerning personal liberty [and] personal security . . . *including the constitutional right to keep and bear arms.*" § 14, 14 Stat. 176 (1866) (emphasis added). That same day, a Bureau official reported that freedmen in Kentucky and Tennessee were still constantly under threat: "No Union man or negro who attempts to take any active part in politics, or the improvement of his race, is safe a single day; and nearly all sleep upon their arms at night, and carry concealed weapons during the day."

Of course, even during Reconstruction the right to keep and bear arms had limits. But those limits were consistent with a right of the public to peaceably carry handguns for self-defense . . . As for Reconstruction-era state regulations, there was little innovation over the kinds of public-carry restrictions that had been commonplace in the early 19th century. . . . Respondents and the United States, however, direct our attention primarily to two late-19th-century cases in Texas [that approved a statutory "reasonable grounds" standard for public carry analogous to New York's proper-cause requirement]

But the Texas statute, and the rationales set forth in [the two cases], are outliers. In fact, only one other State, West Virginia, adopted a similar public-carry statute before 1900. . . . The Texas decisions therefore provide little insight into how postbellum courts viewed the right to carry protected arms in public.

In the end, while we recognize the support that postbellum Texas provides for respondents' view, we will not give disproportionate weight to a single state statute and a pair of state-court decisions. As in *Heller*, we will not "stake our interpretation of the Second Amendment upon a single law, in effect in a single [State], that contradicts the overwhelming weight of other evidence regarding the right to keep and bear arms for defense" in public.

5

Finally, respondents point to the slight uptick in gun regulation during the late-19th century—principally in the Western Territories. As we suggested in *Heller*, however, late-19th-century evidence cannot provide much insight into the meaning of the Second Amendment when it contradicts earlier evidence. . . .

The vast majority of the statutes that respondents invoke come from the Western Territories. . . . [W]e will not stake our interpretation on a handful of temporary territorial laws that were enacted nearly a century after the Second Amendment's adoption, governed less than 1% of the American population, and also "contradic[t] the overwhelming weight" of other, more contemporaneous historical evidence. . . . [In addition,] because these territorial laws were rarely subject to judicial scrutiny, we do not know the basis of their perceived legality. . . .

. . . We will not address any of the 20th-century historical evidence brought to bear by respondents or their amici. As with their late-19th-century evidence, the 20th-century evidence presented by respondents and their amici does not provide insight into the meaning of the Second Amendment when it contradicts earlier evidence. [relocated footnote—eds.]

* * *

At the end of this long journey through the Anglo-American history of public carry, we conclude that respondents have not met their burden to identify an American tradition justifying the State's proper-cause requirement. The Second Amendment guaranteed to "all Americans" the right to bear commonly used arms in public subject to certain reasonable, well-defined restrictions. Those restrictions, for example, limited the intent for which one could carry arms, the manner by which one carried arms, or the exceptional circumstances under which one could not carry arms, such as before justices of the peace and other government officials. Apart from a few late-19th-century outlier jurisdictions, American governments simply have not broadly prohibited the public carry of commonly used firearms for personal defense. Nor, subject to a few late-in-time outliers, have American governments required law-abiding, responsible citizens to "demonstrate a special need for self-protection distinguishable from that of the general community" in order to carry arms in public.

IV

The constitutional right to bear arms in public for self-defense is not "a second-class right, subject to an entirely different body of rules than the other Bill of

Rights guarantees." *McDonald*. We know of no other constitutional right that an individual may exercise only after demonstrating to government officers some special need. That is not how the First Amendment works when it comes to unpopular speech or the free exercise of religion. It is not how the Sixth Amendment works when it comes to a defendant's right to confront the witnesses against him. And it is not how the Second Amendment works when it comes to public carry for self-defense.

New York's proper-cause requirement violates the Fourteenth Amendment in that it prevents law-abiding citizens with ordinary self-defense needs from exercising their right to keep and bear arms. We therefore reverse the judgment of the Court of Appeals and remand the case for further proceedings consistent with this opinion.

It is so ordered.

Justice ALITO, concurring.

I join the opinion of the Court in full but add the following comments in response to the dissent.

Much of the dissent seems designed to obscure the specific question that the Court has decided. . . . [T]he key point that we decided [in *Heller*] was that "the people," not just members of the "militia," have the right to use a firearm to defend themselves. And because many people face a serious risk of lethal violence when they venture outside their homes, the Second Amendment was understood at the time of adoption to apply under those circumstances. The Court's exhaustive historical survey establishes that point very clearly, and today's decision therefore holds that a State may not enforce a law, like New York's Sullivan Law, that effectively prevents its law-abiding residents from carrying a gun for this purpose.

That is all we decide. Our holding decides nothing about who may lawfully possess a firearm or the requirements that must be met to buy a gun. Nor does it decide anything about the kinds of weapons that people may possess. Nor have we disturbed anything that we said in *Heller* or *McDonald*, about restrictions that may be imposed on the possession or carrying of guns.

In light of what we have actually held, it is hard to see what legitimate purpose can possibly be served by most of the dissent's lengthy introductory section. Why, for example, does the dissent think it is relevant to recount the mass shootings that have occurred in recent years? Does the dissent think that laws like New York's prevent or deter such atrocities? Will a person bent on carrying out a mass shooting be stopped if he knows that it is illegal to carry a handgun outside the home? And how does the dissent account for the fact that one of the mass shootings near the top of its list took place in Buffalo? The New York law at issue in this case obviously did not stop that perpetrator.

What is the relevance of statistics about the use of guns to commit suicide? Does the dissent think that a lot of people who possess guns in their homes will be stopped or deterred from shooting themselves if they cannot lawfully take them outside?

The dissent cites statistics about the use of guns in domestic disputes, but it does not explain why these statistics are relevant to the question presented in this case. How many of the cases involving the use of a gun in a domestic dispute occur outside the home, and how many are prevented by laws like New York's?

The dissent cites statistics on children and adolescents killed by guns, but what does this have to do with the question whether an adult who is licensed to possess a handgun may be prohibited from carrying it outside the home? Our decision, as noted, does not expand the categories of people who may lawfully possess a gun, and federal law generally forbids the possession of a handgun by a person who is under the age of 18, and bars the sale of a handgun to anyone under the age of 21.

The dissent cites the large number of guns in private hands—nearly 400 million—but it does not explain what this statistic has to do with the question whether a person who already has the right to keep a gun in the home for self-defense is likely to be deterred from acquiring a gun by the knowledge that the gun cannot be carried outside the home. And while the dissent seemingly thinks that the ubiquity of guns and our country's high level of gun violence provide reasons for sustaining the New York law, the dissent appears not to understand that it is these very facts that cause law-abiding citizens to feel the need to carry a gun for self-defense.

No one apparently knows how many of the 400 million privately held guns are in the hands of criminals, but there can be little doubt that many muggers and rapists are armed and are undeterred by the Sullivan Law. Each year, the New York City Police Department (NYPD) confiscates thousands of guns, and it is fair to assume that the number of guns seized is a fraction of the total number held unlawfully. The police cannot disarm every person who acquires a gun for use in criminal activity; nor can they provide bodyguard protection for the State's nearly 20 million residents or the 8.8 million people who live in New York City. Some of these people live in high-crime neighborhoods. Some must traverse dark and dangerous streets in order to reach their homes after work or other evening activities. Some are members of groups whose members feel especially vulnerable. And some of these people reasonably believe that unless they can brandish or, if necessary, use a handgun in the case of attack, they may be murdered, raped, or suffer some other serious injury.

Ordinary citizens frequently use firearms to protect themselves from criminal attack. According to survey data, defensive firearm use occurs up to 2.5 million times per year. A Centers for Disease Control and Prevention report commissioned by former President Barack Obama reviewed the literature surrounding firearms use and noted that "[s]tudies that directly assessed the effect of actual defensive uses of guns ... have found consistently lower injury rates among gun-using crime victims compared with victims who used other self-protective strategies." ...

I reiterate: All that we decide in this case is that the Second Amendment protects the right of law-abiding people to carry a gun outside the home for self-defense and that the Sullivan Law, which makes that virtually impossible for most New Yorkers, is unconstitutional.

Justice KAVANAUGH, with whom THE CHIEF JUSTICE joins, concurring.
. . .

I join the Court's opinion, and I write separately to underscore two important points about the limits of the Court's decision.

First, the Court's decision does not prohibit States from imposing licensing requirements for carrying a handgun for self-defense. In particular, the Court's decision does not affect the existing licensing regimes—known as "shall-issue" regimes—that are employed in 43 States.

The Court's decision addresses only the unusual discretionary licensing regimes, known as "may-issue" regimes, that are employed by 6 States including New York. As the Court explains, New York's outlier may-issue regime is constitutionally problematic because it grants open-ended discretion to licensing officials and authorizes licenses only for those applicants who can show some special need apart from self-defense. Those features of New York's regime—the unchanneled discretion for licensing officials and the special-need requirement—in effect deny the right to carry handguns for self-defense to many "ordinary, law-abiding citizens.". . .

By contrast, 43 States employ objective shall-issue licensing regimes. Those shall-issue regimes may require a license applicant to undergo fingerprinting, a background check, a mental health records check, and training in firearms handling and in laws regarding the use of force, among other possible requirements. Unlike New York's may-issue regime, those shall-issue regimes do not grant open-ended discretion to licensing officials and do not require a showing of some special need apart from self-defense. As petitioners acknowledge, shall-issue licensing regimes are constitutionally permissible, subject of course to an as-applied challenge if a shall-issue licensing regime does not operate in that manner in practice.

Going forward, therefore, the 43 States that employ objective shall-issue licensing regimes for carrying handguns for self-defense may continue to do so. Likewise, the 6 States including New York potentially affected by today's decision may continue to require licenses for carrying handguns for self-defense so long as those States employ objective licensing requirements like those used by the 43 shall-issue States.

Second, as *Heller* and *McDonald* established and the Court today again explains, the Second Amendment "is neither a regulatory straightjacket nor a regulatory blank check." *Ante*, at ——. Properly interpreted, the Second Amendment allows a "variety" of gun regulations. As Justice Scalia wrote in his opinion for the Court in *Heller*, and Justice ALITO reiterated in relevant part in the principal opinion in *McDonald*:

"Like most rights, the right secured by the Second Amendment is not unlimited. From Blackstone through the 19th-century cases, commentators and courts routinely explained that the right was not a right to keep and carry any weapon whatsoever in any manner whatsoever and for whatever purpose. . . . [N]othing in our opinion should be taken to cast doubt on longstanding prohibitions on the possession of firearms by felons and the mentally ill, or laws forbidding the carrying of firearms in sensitive places such as schools and government buildings, or laws imposing conditions and qualifications on the commercial sale of arms. [Footnote 26: We identify these presumptively lawful regulatory measures only as examples; our list does not purport to be exhaustive.]

"We also recognize another important limitation on the right to keep and carry arms. *Miller* said, as we have explained, that the sorts of weapons protected were those in common use at the time. We think that limitation is fairly supported by the historical tradition of prohibiting the carrying of dangerous and unusual weapons."

* * *

With those additional comments, I join the opinion of the Court.

Justice BARRETT, concurring.

I join the Court's opinion in full. I write separately to highlight two methodological points that the Court does not resolve. First, the Court does not conclusively determine the manner and circumstances in which postratification practice may bear on the original meaning of the Constitution. . . . Second and relatedly, the Court avoids another "ongoing scholarly debate on whether courts should primarily rely on the prevailing understanding of an individual right when the Fourteenth Amendment was ratified in 1868" or when the Bill of Rights was ratified in 1791. Here, the lack of support for New York's law in either period makes it unnecessary to choose between them. But if 1791 is the benchmark, then New York's appeals to Reconstruction-era history would fail for the independent reason that this evidence is simply too late (in addition to too little). . . . So today's decision should not be understood to endorse freewheeling reliance on historical practice from the mid-to-late 19th century to establish the original meaning of the Bill of Rights. On the contrary, the Court is careful to caution "against giving postenactment history more weight than it can rightly bear."

Justice BREYER, with whom Justice SOTOMAYOR and Justice KAGAN join, dissenting.

In 2020, 45,222 Americans were killed by firearms. Since the start of this year (2022), there have been 277 reported mass shootings—an average of more than one per day. Gun violence has now surpassed motor vehicle crashes as the leading cause of death among children and adolescents.

Many States have tried to address some of the dangers of gun violence just described by passing laws that limit, in various ways, who may purchase, carry, or use firearms of different kinds. The Court today severely burdens States' efforts to do so. It invokes the Second Amendment to strike down a New York law regulating the public carriage of concealed handguns. In my view, that decision rests upon several serious mistakes.

First, the Court decides this case on the basis of the pleadings, without the benefit of discovery or an evidentiary record. As a result, it may well rest its decision on a mistaken understanding of how New York's law operates in practice. Second, the Court wrongly limits its analysis to focus nearly exclusively on history. It refuses to consider the government interests that justify a challenged gun regulation, regardless of how compelling those interests may be. The Constitution contains no such limitation, and neither do our precedents. Third, the Court itself demonstrates the practical problems with its history-only approach. In applying that approach to New York's law, the Court fails to correctly identify and analyze the relevant historical facts. Only by ignoring an abundance of historical evidence supporting regulations restricting the public carriage of firearms can the Court conclude that New York's law is not "consistent with the Nation's historical tradition of firearm regulation."

In my view, when courts interpret the Second Amendment, it is constitutionally proper, indeed often necessary, for them to consider the serious dangers and consequences of gun violence that lead States to regulate firearms. . . . At a minimum, I would not strike down the law based only on the pleadings, as the Court does today—without first allowing for the development of an evidentiary record and without considering the State's compelling interest in preventing gun violence. I respectfully dissent.

I

The question before us concerns the extent to which the Second Amendment prevents democratically elected officials from enacting laws to address the serious problem of gun violence. And yet the Court today purports to answer that question without discussing the nature or severity of that problem.

In 2017, there were an estimated 393.3 million civilian-held firearms in the United States, or about 120 firearms per 100 people. That is more guns per capita than in any other country in the world. (By comparison, Yemen is second with about 52.8 firearms per 100 people—less than half the per capita rate in the United States—and some countries, like Indonesia and Japan, have fewer than one firearm per 100 people.)

Unsurprisingly, the United States also suffers a disproportionately high rate of firearm-related deaths and injuries. In 2015, approximately 36,000 people were killed by firearms nationwide. Of those deaths, 22,018 (or about 61%) were suicides, 13,463 (37%) were homicides, and 489 (1%) were unintentional injuries. On top of that, firearms caused an average of 85,694 emergency room visits for nonfatal injuries each year between 2009 and 2017.

Worse yet, gun violence appears to be on the rise. By 2020, the number of firearm-related deaths had risen to 45,222, or by about 25% since 2015. That means that, in 2020, an average of about 124 people died from gun violence every day. As I mentioned above, gun violence has now become the leading cause of death in children and adolescents, surpassing car crashes, which had previously been the leading cause of death in that age group for over 60 years.

And the consequences of gun violence are borne disproportionately by communities of color, and Black communities in particular.

The dangers posed by firearms can take many forms. Newspapers report mass shootings occurring at an entertainment district in Philadelphia, Pennsylvania (3 dead and 11 injured); an elementary school in Uvalde, Texas (21 dead); a supermarket in Buffalo, New York (10 dead and 3 injured); a series of spas in Atlanta, Georgia (8 dead); a busy street in an entertainment district of Dayton, Ohio (9 dead and 17 injured); a nightclub in Orlando, Florida (50 dead and 53 injured); a church in Charleston, South Carolina (9 dead); a movie theater in Aurora, Colorado (12 dead and 50 injured); an elementary school in Newtown, Connecticut (26 dead); and many, many more. Since the start of this year alone (2022), there have already been 277 reported mass shootings—an average of more than one per day.

And mass shootings are just one part of the problem. Easy access to firearms can also make many other aspects of American life more dangerous. Consider, for example, the effect of guns on road rage. In 2021, an average of 44 people each month were shot and either killed or wounded in road rage incidents, double the annual average between 2016 and 2019. Some of those deaths might have been avoided if there had not been a loaded gun in the car.

The same could be said of protests: A study of 30,000 protests between January 2020 and June 2021 found that armed protests were nearly six times more likely to become violent or destructive than unarmed protests. Or domestic disputes: Another study found that a woman is five times more likely to be killed by an abusive partner if that partner has access to a gun. Or suicides: A study found that men who own handguns are three times as likely to commit suicide than men who do not and women who own handguns are seven times as likely to commit suicide than women who do not.

Consider, too, interactions with police officers. The presence of a gun in the hands of a civilian poses a risk to both officers and civilians. *Amici* prosecutors and police chiefs tell us that most officers who are killed in the line of duty are killed by firearms; they explain that officers in States with high rates of gun ownership are three times as likely to be killed in the line of duty as officers in States with low rates of gun ownership. They also say that States with the highest rates of gun ownership report four times as many fatal shootings of civilians by police officers compared to States with the lowest rates of gun ownership.

These are just some examples of the dangers that firearms pose. There is, of course, another side to the story. I am not simply saying that "guns are bad." Some Americans use guns for legitimate purposes, such as sport (*e.g.,* hunting or target shooting), certain types of employment (*e.g.,* as a private security guard), or self-defense. Balancing these lawful uses against the dangers of firearms is primarily the responsibility of elected bodies, such as legislatures. It requires consideration of facts, statistics, expert opinions, predictive judgments, relevant values, and a host of other circumstances, which together make decisions about how, when, and where to regulate guns more appropriately legislative work. That consideration counsels modesty and restraint on the part of judges when they interpret and apply the Second Amendment.

Consider, for one thing, that different types of firearms may pose different risks and serve different purposes. The Court has previously observed that handguns, the type of firearm at issue here, "are the most popular weapon chosen by Americans for self-defense in the home." *Heller*. But handguns are also the most popular weapon chosen by perpetrators of violent crimes. In 2018, 64.4% of firearm homicides and 91.8% of nonfatal firearm assaults were committed with a handgun. Handguns are also the most commonly stolen type of firearm — 63% of burglaries resulting in gun theft between 2005 and 2010 involved the theft of at least one handgun.

Or consider, for another thing, that the dangers and benefits posed by firearms may differ between urban and rural areas. Firearm-related homicides and assaults are significantly more common in urban areas than rural ones. For example, from 1999 to 2016, 89.8% of the 213,175 firearm-related homicides in the United States occurred in "metropolitan" areas.

Justice ALITO asks why I have begun my opinion by reviewing some of the dangers and challenges posed by gun violence and what relevance that has to today's case. All of the above considerations illustrate that the question of firearm regulation presents a complex problem — one that should be solved by legislatures rather than courts. What kinds of firearm regulations should a State adopt? Different States might choose to answer that question differently. They may face different challenges because of their different geographic and demographic compositions. A State like New York, which must account for the roughly 8.5 million people living in the 303 square miles of New York City, might choose to adopt different (and stricter) firearms regulations than States like Montana or Wyoming, which do not contain any city remotely comparable in terms of population or density. For a variety of reasons, States may also be willing to tolerate different degrees of risk and therefore choose to balance the competing benefits and dangers of firearms differently.

The question presented in this case concerns the extent to which the Second Amendment restricts different States (and the Federal Government) from working out solutions to these problems through democratic processes. The primary difference between the Court's view and mine is that I believe the Amendment allows States to take account of the serious problems posed by gun violence that I have just described. I fear that the Court's interpretation ignores these significant dangers and leaves States without the ability to address them.

II

[The Court] suggests that New York's licensing regime gives licensing officers too much discretion and provides too "limited" judicial review of their decisions, that the proper cause standard is too "demanding," and that these features make New York an outlier compared to the "vast majority of States,". But on what evidence does the Court base these characterizations? Recall that this case comes to us at the pleading stage. The parties have not had an opportunity to conduct discovery, and no evidentiary hearings have been held to develop the record. Thus, at this point, there is no record to support the Court's negative characterizations, as we know very little about how the law has actually been applied on the ground. . . .

[T]he Court compares New York's licensing regime to that of other States. It says that New York's law is a "may issue" licensing regime, which the Court describes as a law that provides licensing officers greater discretion to grant or deny licenses than a "shall issue" licensing regime. Because the Court counts 43 "shall issue" jurisdictions and only 7 "may issue" jurisdictions, it suggests that New York's law is an outlier. Implicitly, the Court appears to ask, if so many other States have adopted the more generous "shall issue" approach, why can New York not be required to do the same?

[I]n drawing a line between "may issue" and "shall issue" licensing regimes, the Court ignores the degree of variation within and across these categories. Not all "may issue" regimes are necessarily alike, nor are all "shall issue" regimes. Conversely, not all "may issue" regimes are as different from the "shall issue" regimes as the Court assumes. . . . [Some states classified as "shall issue" have discretionary criteria in their statutes or grant some degree of discretionary licensing to authorities.] [T]he line between "may issue" and "shall issue" regimes is not as clear cut as the Court suggests, and that line depends at least in part on how statutory discretion is applied in practice. Here, because the Court strikes down New York's law without affording the State an opportunity to develop an evidentiary record, we do not know how much discretion licensing officers in New York have in practice or how that discretion is exercised, let alone how the licensing regimes in the other six "may issue" jurisdictions operate.

"[S]hall issue" licensing regimes are a relatively recent development. Until the 1980s, "may issue" regimes predominated. As of 1987, 16 States and the District of Columbia prohibited concealed carriage outright, 26 States had "may issue" licensing regimes, 7 States had "shall issue" regimes, and 1 State (Vermont) allowed concealed carriage without a permit. Thus, it has only been in the last few decades that States have shifted toward "shall issue" licensing laws. Prior to that, most States operated "may issue" licensing regimes without legal or practical problem.

[B]y the Court's count, the seven "may issue" jurisdictions are New York, California, Hawaii, Maryland, Massachusetts, New Jersey, and the District of Columbia. Together, these seven jurisdictions comprise about 84.4 million people and account for over a quarter of the country's population. Thus, "may issue" laws can hardly be described as a marginal or outdated regime.

And there are good reasons why these seven jurisdictions may have chosen not to follow other States in shifting toward "shall issue" regimes. The seven remaining "may issue" jurisdictions are among the most densely populated in the United States [and] contain some of the country's densest and most populous urban areas, *e.g.,* New York City, Los Angeles, San Francisco, the District of

Columbia, Honolulu, and Boston. . . . [D]ensely populated urban areas face different kinds and degrees of dangers from gun violence than rural areas. It is thus easy to see why the seven "may issue" jurisdictions might choose to regulate firearm carriage more strictly than other States.

New York and its *amici* present substantial data justifying the State's decision to retain a "may issue" licensing regime. The data show that stricter gun regulations are associated with lower rates of firearm-related death and injury. In particular, studies have shown that "may issue" licensing regimes, like New York's, are associated with lower homicide rates and lower violent crime rates than "shall issue" licensing regimes. For example, one study compared homicide rates across all 50 States during the 25-year period from 1991 to 2015 and found that "shall issue" laws were associated with 6.5% higher total homicide rates, 8.6% higher firearm homicide rates, and 10.6% higher handgun homicide rates. Another study longitudinally followed 33 States that had adopted "shall-issue" laws between 1981 and 2007 and found that the adoption of those laws was associated with a 13%-15% increase in rates of violent crime after 10 years. . . .

Justice ALITO points to competing empirical evidence that arrives at a different conclusion. . . . But these types of disagreements are exactly the sort that are better addressed by legislatures than courts. The Court today restricts the ability of legislatures to fulfill that role. It does so without knowing how New York's law is administered in practice, how much discretion licensing officers in New York possess, or whether the proper cause standard differs across counties. And it does so without giving the State an opportunity to develop the evidentiary record to answer those questions. Yet it strikes down New York's licensing regime as a violation of the Second Amendment.

III

A

How does the Court justify striking down New York's law without first considering how it actually works on the ground and what purposes it serves? The Court does so by purporting to rely nearly exclusively on history. It requires "the government [to] affirmatively prove that its firearms regulation is part of the historical tradition that delimits the outer bounds of 'the right to keep and bear arms.'" *Ante,* at ——. Beyond this historical inquiry, the Court refuses to employ what it calls "means-end scrutiny." That is, it refuses to consider whether New York has a compelling interest in regulating the concealed carriage of handguns or whether New York's law is narrowly tailored to achieve that interest. Although I agree that history can often be a useful tool in determining the meaning and scope of constitutional provisions, I believe the Court's near-exclusive reliance on that single tool today goes much too far.

The Court concedes that no Court of Appeals has adopted its rigid history-only approach. To the contrary, every Court of Appeals to have addressed the question has agreed on a two-step framework for evaluating whether a firearm regulation is consistent with the Second Amendment. At the first step, the Courts of Appeals use text and history to determine "whether the regulated activity falls within the scope of the Second Amendment." If it does, they go on to the second step and consider " 'the strength of the government's justification for restricting or regulating' " the Second Amendment right. In doing so, they apply a level of "means-ends" scrutiny "that is proportionate to the severity of the burden that the law imposes on the right": strict scrutiny if the burden is severe, and intermediate scrutiny if it is not.

The Court today replaces the Courts of Appeals' consensus framework with its own history-only approach. That is unusual. We do not normally disrupt settled consensus among the Courts of Appeals, especially not when that consensus approach has been applied without issue for over a decade. The Court attempts to justify its deviation from our normal practice by claiming that the Courts of Appeals' approach is inconsistent with *Heller*. In doing so, the Court implies that all 11 Courts of Appeals that have considered this question misread *Heller*.

To the contrary, it is this Court that misreads *Heller*. [*Heller*] . . . faulted my dissent for proposing "a *freestanding* 'interest-balancing' approach" that accorded with "*none of the traditionally expressed levels* [of scrutiny] (strict scrutiny, intermediate scrutiny, rational basis)." (emphasis added). . . . "We know of no other enumerated constitutional right whose core protection has been subjected to a freestanding 'interest-balancing' approach." *Ibid.* To illustrate this point, it cited as an example the First Amendment right to free speech. Judges, of course, regularly use means-end scrutiny, including both strict and intermediate scrutiny, when they interpret or apply the First Amendment. The majority therefore cannot have intended its opinion, consistent with our First Amendment jurisprudence, to be read as rejecting all traditional forms of means-end scrutiny.

[T]he Court today is wrong when it says that its rejection of means-end scrutiny and near-exclusive focus on history "accords with how we protect other constitutional rights." [W]e do look to history in the First Amendment context to determine "whether the expressive conduct falls outside of the category of protected speech." But, if conduct falls within a category of protected speech, we then use means-end scrutiny to determine whether a challenged regulation unconstitutionally burdens that speech. And the degree of scrutiny we apply often depends on the type of speech burdened and the severity of the burden. See, *e.g., Arizona Free Enterprise Club's Freedom Club PAC v. Bennett*, 564 U.S. 721, 734 (2011) (applying strict scrutiny to laws that burden political speech); *Ward v. Rock Against Racism*, 491 U.S. 781, 791 (1989) (applying intermediate scrutiny to time, place, and manner restrictions); *Central Hudson Gas & Elec. Corp. v. Public Serv. Comm'n of N. Y.*, 447 U.S. 557, 564-566 (1980) (applying intermediate scrutiny to laws that burden commercial speech).

Additionally, beyond the right to freedom of speech, we regularly use means-end scrutiny in cases involving other constitutional provisions. See, *e.g., Church of Lukumi Babalu Aye, Inc. v. Hialeah*, 508 U.S. 520, 546 (1993) (applying strict scrutiny under the First Amendment to laws that restrict free exercise of religion in a way that is not neutral and generally applicable); *Adarand Constructors,*

Inc. v. Peña, 515 U.S. 200, 227 (1995) (applying strict scrutiny under the Equal Protection Clause to race-based classifications); *Clark v. Jeter*, 486 U.S. 456, 461 (1988) (applying intermediate scrutiny under the Equal Protection Clause to sex-based classifications); see also *Virginia v. Moore*, 553 U.S. 164, 171 (2008) ("When history has not provided a conclusive answer, we have analyzed a search or seizure in light of traditional standards of reasonableness").

The upshot is that applying means-end scrutiny to laws that regulate the Second Amendment right to bear arms would not create a constitutional anomaly. Rather, it is the Court's rejection of means-end scrutiny and adoption of a rigid history-only approach that is anomalous.

B

The Court's near-exclusive reliance on history is not only unnecessary, it is deeply impractical. It imposes a task on the lower courts that judges cannot easily accomplish. Judges understand well how to weigh a law's objectives (its "ends") against the methods used to achieve those objectives (its "means"). Judges are far less accustomed to resolving difficult historical questions. Courts are, after all, staffed by lawyers, not historians. Legal experts typically have little experience answering contested historical questions or applying those answers to resolve contemporary problems.

The Court's insistence that judges and lawyers rely nearly exclusively on history to interpret the Second Amendment thus raises a host of troubling questions. Consider, for example, the following. Do lower courts have the research resources necessary to conduct exhaustive historical analyses in every Second Amendment case? What historical regulations and decisions qualify as representative analogues to modern laws? How will judges determine which historians have the better view of close historical questions? Will the meaning of the Second Amendment change if or when new historical evidence becomes available? And, most importantly, will the Court's approach permit judges to reach the outcomes they prefer and then cloak those outcomes in the language of history? See S. Cornell, *Heller*, New Originalism, and Law Office History: "Meet the New Boss, Same as the Old Boss," 56 UCLA L. Rev. 1095, 1098 (2009) (describing "law office history" as "a results oriented methodology in which evidence is selectively gathered and interpreted to produce a preordained conclusion").

Consider *Heller* itself. That case, fraught with difficult historical questions, illustrates the practical problems with expecting courts to decide important constitutional questions based solely on history. The majority in *Heller* undertook 40 pages of textual and historical analysis and concluded that the Second Amendment's protection of the right to "keep and bear Arms" historically encompassed an "individual right to possess and carry weapons in case of confrontation" — that is, for self-defense. Justice Stevens' dissent conducted an equally searching textual and historical inquiry and concluded, to the contrary, that the term "bear Arms" was an idiom that protected only the right "to use and possess arms in conjunction with service in a well-regulated militia." I do not intend to relitigate *Heller* here. I accept its holding as a matter of *stare decisis*.

I refer to its historical analysis only to show the difficulties inherent in answering historical questions and to suggest that judges do not have the expertise needed to answer those questions accurately.

For example, the *Heller* majority relied heavily on its interpretation of the English Bill of Rights. Citing Blackstone, the majority claimed that the English Bill of Rights protected a " 'right of having and using arms for self-preservation and defence.' " (quoting 1 Commentaries on the Laws of England 140 (1765)). The majority interpreted that language to mean a private right to bear arms for self-defense, "having nothing whatever to do with service in a militia." Two years later, however, 21 English and early American historians (including experts at top universities) told us in *McDonald v. Chicago*, that the *Heller* Court had gotten the history wrong: The English Bill of Rights "did not . . . protect an individual's right to possess, own, or use arms for private purposes such as to defend a home against burglars." Brief for English/Early American Historians as *Amici Curiae* in *McDonald v. Chicago*, O. T. 2009, No. 081521, p. 2. Rather, these *amici* historians explained, the English right to "have arms" ensured that the Crown could not deny Parliament (which represented the people) the power to arm the landed gentry and raise a militia—or the right of the people to possess arms to take part in that militia— "should the sovereign usurp the laws, liberties, estates, and Protestant religion of the nation." Thus, the English right did protect a right of "self-preservation and defence," as Blackstone said, but that right "was to be exercised not by individuals acting privately or independently, but as a militia organized by their elected representatives," *i.e.,* Parliament. The Court, not an expert in history, had misread Blackstone and other sources explaining the English Bill of Rights.

And that was not the *Heller* Court's only questionable judgment. The majority rejected Justice Stevens' argument that the Second Amendment's use of the words "bear Arms" drew on an idiomatic meaning that, at the time of the founding, commonly referred to military service. 554 U.S. at 586, 128 S.Ct. 2783. Linguistics experts now tell us that the majority was wrong to do so. See, *e.g.,* Brief for Corpus Linguistics Professors and Experts as *Amici Curiae* (Brief for Linguistics Professors); Brief for Neal Goldfarb as *Amicus Curiae*; Brief for Americans Against Gun Violence as *Amicus Curiae* 13-15. Since *Heller* was decided, experts have searched over 120,000 founding-era texts from between 1760 and 1799, as well as 40,000 texts from sources dating as far back as 1475, for historical uses of the phrase "bear arms," and they concluded that the phrase was overwhelmingly used to refer to " 'war, soldiering, or other forms of armed action by a group rather than an individual.' " Brief for Linguistics Professors 11, 14; see also D. Baron, Corpus Evidence Illuminates the Meaning of Bear Arms, 46 Hastings Const. L. Q. 509, 510 (2019) ("Non-military uses of *bear arms* in reference to hunting or personal self-defense are not just rare, they are almost nonexistent"); *id.*, at 510-511 (reporting 900 instances in which "bear arms" was used to refer to military or collective use of firearms and only 7 instances that were either ambiguous or without a military connotation).

These are just two examples. Other scholars have continued to write books and articles arguing that the Court's decision in *Heller* misread the text and history of the Second Amendment. See generally, *e.g.,* M. Waldman, The Second Amendment (2014); S. Cornell, The Changing Meaning of the Right To Keep and Bear Arms: 1688–1788, in Guns in Law 20-27 (A. Sarat, L. Douglas, & M. Umphrey eds. 2019); P. Finkelman, The Living Constitution and the Second Amendment: Poor History, False Originalism, and a Very Confused Court, 37 Cardozo L. Rev. 623 (2015); D. Walker, Necessary to the Security of Free States: The Second Amendment as the Auxiliary Right of Federalism, 56 Am. J. Legal Hist. 365 (2016); W. Merkel, *Heller* as Hubris, and How *McDonald v. City of Chicago* May Well Change the Constitutional World as We Know It, 50 Santa Clara L. Rev. 1221 (2010).

I repeat that I do not cite these arguments in order to relitigate *Heller.* I wish only to illustrate the difficulties that may befall lawyers and judges when they attempt to rely *solely* on history to interpret the Constitution. In *Heller,* we attempted to determine the scope of the Second Amendment right to bear arms by conducting a historical analysis, and some of us arrived at very different conclusions based on the same historical sources. Many experts now tell us that the Court got it wrong in a number of ways. That is understandable given the difficulty of the inquiry that the Court attempted to undertake. The Court's past experience with historical analysis should serve as a warning against relying exclusively, or nearly exclusively, on this mode of analysis in the future.

Failing to heed that warning, the Court today does just that. Its near-exclusive reliance on history will pose a number of practical problems. First, the difficulties attendant to extensive historical analysis will be especially acute in the lower courts. The Court's historical analysis in this case is over 30 pages long and reviews numerous original sources from over 600 years of English and American history. Lower courts—especially district courts—typically have fewer research resources, less assistance from *amici* historians, and higher caseloads than we do. They are therefore ill equipped to conduct the type of searching historical surveys that the Court's approach requires. Tellingly, even the Courts of Appeals that have addressed the question presented here (namely, the constitutionality of public carriage restrictions like New York's) "have, in large part, avoided extensive historical analysis." *Young v. Hawaii,* 992 F.3d 765, 784-785 (CA9 2021) (collecting cases). In contrast, lawyers and courts are well equipped to administer means-end scrutiny, which is regularly applied in a variety of constitutional contexts.

Second, the Court's opinion today compounds these problems, for it gives the lower courts precious little guidance regarding how to resolve modern constitutional questions based almost solely on history. The Court declines to "provide an exhaustive survey of the features that render regulations relevantly similar under the Second Amendment." Other than noting that its history-only analysis is "neither a . . . straightjacket nor a . . . blank check," the Court offers little explanation of how stringently its test should be applied. Ironically, the only two "relevan[t]" metrics that the Court does identify are "how and why" a gun control regulation "burden[s the] right to armed self-defense." In other words, the Court believes that the most relevant metrics of comparison are a regulation's means (how) and ends (why)—even as it rejects the utility of means-end scrutiny.

What the Court offers instead is a laundry list of reasons to discount seemingly relevant historical evidence. The Court believes that some historical laws and decisions cannot justify upholding modern regulations because, it says, they were outliers. It explains that just two court decisions or three colonial laws are not enough to satisfy its test. But the Court does not say how many cases or laws would suffice "to show a tradition of public-carry regulation." Other laws are irrelevant, the Court claims, because they are too dissimilar from New York's concealed-carry licensing regime. But the Court does not say what "representative historical analogue," short of a "twin" or a "dead ringer," would suffice. Indeed, the Court offers many and varied reasons to reject potential representative analogues, but very few reasons to accept them. At best, the numerous justifications that the Court finds for rejecting historical evidence give judges ample tools to pick their friends out of history's crowd. At worst, they create a one-way ratchet that will disqualify virtually any "representative historical analogue" and make it nearly impossible to sustain common-sense regulations necessary to our Nation's safety and security.

Third, even under ideal conditions, historical evidence will often fail to provide clear answers to difficult questions. As an initial matter, many aspects of the history of firearms and their regulation are ambiguous, contradictory, or disputed. Unsurprisingly, the extent to which colonial statutes enacted over 200 years ago were actually enforced, the basis for an acquittal in a 17th-century decision, and the interpretation of English laws from the Middle Ages (to name just a few examples) are often less than clear. And even historical experts may reach conflicting conclusions based on the same sources. As a result, history, as much as any other interpretive method, leaves ample discretion to "loo[k] over the heads of the [crowd] for one's friends." A. Scalia & B. Garner, Reading Law: The Interpretation of Legal Texts 377 (2012).

Fourth, I fear that history will be an especially inadequate tool when it comes to modern cases presenting modern problems. Consider the Court's apparent preference for founding-era regulation. Our country confronted profoundly different problems during that time period than it does today. Society at the founding was "predominantly rural." In 1790, most of America's relatively small population of just four million people lived on farms or in small towns. Even New York City, the largest American city then, as it is now, had a population of just 33,000 people. Small founding-era towns are unlikely to have faced the same degrees and types of risks from gun violence as major metropolitan areas do today, so the types of regulations they adopted are unlikely to address modern needs.

This problem is all the more acute when it comes to "modern-day circumstances that [the Framers] could not have anticipated." How can we expect laws and cases that are over a century old to dictate the legality of regulations targeting "ghost guns" constructed with the aid of a three-dimensional printer? Or modern laws requiring all gun shops to offer smart guns, which can only be fired by authorized users? Or laws imposing additional criminal penalties for the use of bullets capable of piercing body armor?

The Court's answer is that judges will simply have to employ "analogical reasoning." But, as I explained above, the Court does not provide clear guidance on how to apply such reasoning. Even seemingly straightforward historical restrictions on firearm use may prove surprisingly difficult to apply to modern circumstances. The Court affirms *Heller*'s recognition that States may forbid public carriage in "sensitive places." But what, in 21st-century New York City, may properly be considered a sensitive place? Presumably "legislative assemblies, polling places, and courthouses," which the Court tells us were among the "relatively few" places "where weapons were altogether prohibited" in the 18th and 19th centuries. On the other hand, the Court also tells us that "expanding the category of 'sensitive places' simply to all places of public congregation that are not isolated from law enforcement defines th[at] category . . . far too broadly." So where does that leave the many locations in a modern city with no obvious 18th- or 19th-century analogue? What about subways, nightclubs, movie theaters, and sports stadiums? The Court does not say.

Although I hope—fervently—that future courts will be able to identify historical analogues supporting the validity of regulations that address new technologies, I fear that it will often prove difficult to identify analogous technological and social problems from Medieval England, the founding era, or the time period in which the Fourteenth Amendment was ratified. Laws addressing repeating crossbows, launcegays, dirks, dagges, skeines, stilladers, and other ancient weapons will be of little help to courts confronting modern problems. And as technological progress pushes our society ever further beyond the bounds of the Framers' imaginations, attempts at "analogical reasoning" will become increasingly tortured. In short, a standard that relies solely on history is unjustifiable and unworkable.

IV

Indeed, the Court's application of its history-only test in this case demonstrates the very pitfalls described above. The historical evidence reveals a 700-year Anglo-American tradition of regulating the public carriage of firearms in general, and concealed or concealable firearms in particular. The Court spends more than half of its opinion trying to discredit this tradition. But, in my view, the robust evidence of such a tradition cannot be so easily explained away. Laws regulating the public carriage of weapons existed in England as early as the 13th century and on this Continent since before the founding. Similar laws remained on the books through the ratifications of the Second and Fourteenth Amendments through to the present day. Many of those historical regulations imposed significantly stricter restrictions on public carriage than New York's licensing requirements do today. Thus, even applying the Court's history-only analysis, New York's law must be upheld because "historical precedent from before, during, and . . . after the founding evinces a comparable tradition of regulation."

A. ENGLAND.

[T]he relevant English history begins in the late-13th and early-14th centuries, when Edward I and Edward II issued a series of orders to local sheriffs that prohibited any person from "going armed." . . . . Violators were subject to punishment, including "forfeiture of life and limb." Many of these royal edicts contained exemptions for persons who had obtained "the king's special licence." Like New York's law, these early edicts prohibited public carriage absent special governmental permission and enforced that prohibition on pain of punishment.

The Court seems to suggest that these early regulations are irrelevant because they were enacted during a time of "turmoil" when "malefactors . . . harried the country, committing assaults and murders." But it would seem to me that what the Court characterizes as a "right of armed self-defense" would be more, rather than less, necessary during a time of "turmoil." The Court also suggests that laws that were enacted before firearms arrived in England, like these early edicts and the subsequent Statute of Northampton, are irrelevant. But why should that be? Pregun regulations prohibiting "going armed" in public illustrate an entrenched tradition of restricting public carriage of weapons. That tradition seems as likely to apply to firearms as to any other lethal weapons — particularly if we follow the Court's instruction to use analogical reasoning. And indeed, as we shall shortly see, the most significant prefirearm regulation of public carriage — the Statute of Northampton — was in fact applied to guns once they appeared in England. . . .

The Court thinks that the Statute of Northampton "has little bearing on the Second Amendment," in part because it was "enacted . . . more than 450 years before the ratification of the Constitution." The statute, however, remained in force for hundreds of years, well into the 18th century. It was discussed in the writings of Blackstone, Coke, and others. And several American Colonies and States enacted restrictions modeled on the statute. There is thus every reason to believe that the Framers of the Second Amendment would have considered the Statute of Northampton a significant chapter in the Anglo-American tradition of firearms regulation.

The Court also believes that, by the end of the 17th century, the Statute of Northampton was understood to contain an extratextual intent element: the intent to cause terror in others. . . . But other sources suggest that carrying arms in public was prohibited *because* it naturally tended to terrify the people. . . . According to these sources, terror was the natural consequence — not an additional element — of the crime. . . . Although the Statute of Northampton is particularly significant because of its breadth, longevity, and impact on American law, it was far from the only English restriction on firearms or their carriage. . . . Whatever right to bear arms we inherited from our English forebears, it was qualified by a robust tradition of public carriage regulations.

As I have made clear, I am not a historian. But if the foregoing facts, which historians and other scholars have presented to us, are even roughly correct, it is difficult to see how the Court can believe that English history fails to support legal restrictions on the public carriage of firearms.

B. THE COLONIES.

The American Colonies continued the English tradition of regulating public carriage on this side of the Atlantic. . . . It is true, as the Court points out, that these laws were only enacted in three colonies. But that does not mean that they may be dismissed as outliers. They were successors to several centuries of comparable laws in England, and predecessors to numerous similar (in some cases, materially identical) laws enacted by the States after the founding. And while it may be true that these laws applied only to "dangerous and unusual weapons," that category almost certainly included guns. Finally, the Court points out that New Jersey's ban on public carriage applied only to certain people or to the concealed carriage of certain smaller firearms. But the Court's refusal to credit the relevance of East New Jersey's law on this basis raises a serious question about what, short of a "twin" or a "dead ringer," qualifies as a relevant historical analogue.

C. THE FOUNDING ERA.

The tradition of regulations restricting public carriage of firearms, inherited from England and adopted by the Colonies, continued into the founding era. Virginia, for example, enacted a law in 1786 that, like the Statute of Northampton, prohibited any person from "go[ing] nor rid[ing] armed by night nor by day, in fairs or markets, or in other places, in terror of the Country." And, as the Court acknowledges, "public-carry restrictions proliferate[d]" after the Second Amendment's ratification five years later in 1791. Just a year after that, North Carolina enacted a law whose language was lifted from the Statute of Northampton virtually verbatim (vestigial references to the King included). Other States passed similar laws in the late-18th and 19th centuries.

The Court discounts these laws primarily because they were modeled on the Statute of Northampton, which it believes prohibited only public carriage with the intent to terrify. I have previously explained why I believe that preventing public terror was one *reason* that the Statute of Northampton prohibited public carriage, but not an *element* of the crime. And, consistent with that understanding, American regulations modeled on the Statute of Northampton appear to have been understood to set forth a broad prohibition on public carriage of firearms without any intent-to-terrify requirement. . . . The founding-era regulations—like the colonial and English laws on which they were modeled—thus demonstrate a longstanding tradition of broad restrictions on public carriage of firearms.

D. THE 19TH CENTURY.

Beginning in the 19th century, States began to innovate on the Statute of Northampton in at least two ways. First, many States and Territories passed bans on concealed carriage or on any carriage, concealed or otherwise, of certain concealable weapons. For example, Georgia made it unlawful to carry, "unless in an open manner and fully exposed to view, any pistol, (except horseman's pistols,) dirk, sword in a cane, spear, bowie-knife, or any other kind of knives, manufactured and sold for the purpose of offence and defence." Other States and Territories enacted similar prohibitions. And the Territory of New Mexico appears to have banned all carriage whatsoever of "any class of pistols whatever," as well as "bowie kni[ves,] . . . Arkansas toothpick[s], Spanish dagger[s], slung-shot[s], or any other deadly weapon." These 19th-century bans on concealed carriage were stricter than New York's law, for they prohibited concealed carriage with at most limited exceptions, while New York permits concealed carriage with a lawfully obtained license. Moreover, as *Heller* recognized, and the Court acknowledges, "the majority of the 19th-century courts to consider the question held that [these types of] prohibitions on carrying concealed weapons *were lawful* under the Second Amendment or state analogues."

The Court discounts this history because, it says, courts in four Southern States suggested or held that a ban on concealed carriage was only lawful if open carriage or carriage of military pistols was allowed. . . . Several of these decisions, however, emphasized States' leeway to regulate firearms carriage as necessary "to protect the orderly and well disposed citizens from the treacherous use of weapons not even designed for any purpose of public defence." . . . And other courts upheld concealed-carry restrictions without any reference to an exception allowing open carriage, so it is far from clear that the cases the Court cites represent a consensus view. . . . And, of course, the Court does not say whether the result in this case would be different if New York allowed open carriage by law-abiding citizens as a matter of course.

The second 19th-century innovation, adopted in a number of States, was surety laws. Massachusetts' surety law, which served as a model for laws adopted by many other States, provided that any person who went "armed with a dirk, dagger, sword, pistol, or other offensive and dangerous weapon," and who lacked "reasonable cause to fear an assualt [*sic*]," could be made to pay a surety upon the "complaint of any person having reasonable cause to fear an injury, or breach of the peace." Other States and Territories enacted identical or substantially similar laws. These laws resemble New York's licensing regime in many, though admittedly not all, relevant respects. Most notably, like New York's proper cause requirement, the surety laws conditioned public carriage in at least some circumstances on a special showing of need.

The Court believes that the absence of recorded cases involving surety laws means that they were rarely enforced. Of course, this may just as well show that these laws were normally followed. . . . The surety laws and broader bans on concealed carriage enacted in the 19th century demonstrate that even relatively stringent restrictions on public carriage have long been understood to be consistent with the Second Amendment and its state equivalents.

E. POSTBELLUM REGULATION.

After the Civil War, public carriage of firearms remained subject to extensive regulation. Of course, during this period, Congress provided (and commentators recognized) that firearm regulations could not be designed or enforced in a discriminatory manner. But that by-now uncontroversial proposition says little about the validity of nondiscriminatory restrictions on public carriage, like New York's.

What is more relevant for our purposes is the fact that, in the postbellum period, States continued to enact generally applicable restrictions on public carriage, many of which were even more restrictive than their predecessors. Most notably, many States and Western Territories enacted stringent regulations that prohibited *any* public carriage of firearms, with only limited exceptions. For example, Texas made it a misdemeanor to carry in public "any pistol, dirk, dagger, slung-shot, sword-cane, spear, brass-knuckles, bowie-knife, or any other kind of knife manufactured or sold for the purpose of offense or defense" absent "reasonable grounds for fearing an [immediate and pressing] unlawful attack." Similarly, New Mexico made it "unlawful for any person to carry deadly weapons, either concealed or otherwise, on or about their persons within any of the settlements of this Territory." New Mexico's prohibition contained only narrow exceptions for carriage on a person's own property, for self-defense in the face of immediate danger, or with official authorization. Other States and Territories adopted similar laws.

When they were challenged, these laws were generally upheld. . . . The Court's principal answer to these broad prohibitions on public carriage is to discount gun control laws passed in the American West. It notes that laws enacted in the Western Territories were "rarely subject to judicial scrutiny." But, of course, that may well mean that "[w]e . . . can assume it settled that these" regulations were "consistent with the Second Amendment." The Court also reasons that laws enacted in the Western Territories applied to a relatively small portion of the population and were comparatively short lived. But even assuming that is true, it does not mean that these laws were historical aberrations. To the contrary, bans on public carriage in the American West and elsewhere constitute just one chapter of the centuries-old tradition of comparable firearms regulations described above.

F. THE 20TH CENTURY.

The Court disregards "20th-century historical evidence." But it is worth noting that the law the Court strikes down today is well over 100 years old, having been enacted in 1911 and amended to substantially its present form in 1913. That alone gives it a longer historical pedigree than at least three of the four types of firearms regulations that *Heller* identified as "presumptively lawful." see C. Larson, Four Exceptions in Search of a Theory: *District of Columbia v. Heller* and Judicial *Ipse Dixit*, 60 Hastings L.J. 1371, 1374-1379 (2009) (concluding that " 'prohibitions on the possession of firearms by felons and the mentally ill [and] laws imposing conditions and qualifications on the commercial sale of arms' " have their origins in the 20th century). Like Justice KAVANAUGH, I understand the Court's opinion today to cast no doubt on that aspect of *Heller*'s holding. But unlike Justice KAVANAUGH, I find the disconnect between *Heller*'s treatment of laws prohibiting, for example, firearms possession by felons or the mentally ill, and the Court's treatment of New York's licensing regime, hard to square. The inconsistency suggests that the Court today takes either an unnecessarily cramped view of the relevant historical record or a needlessly rigid approach to analogical reasoning.

* * *

The historical examples of regulations similar to New York's licensing regime are legion. Closely analogous English laws were enacted beginning in the 13th century, and similar American regulations were passed during the colonial period, the founding era, the 19th century, and the 20th century. Not all of these laws were identical to New York's, but that is inevitable in an analysis that demands examination of seven centuries of history. At a minimum, the laws I have recounted *resembled* New York's law, similarly restricting the right to publicly carry weapons and serving roughly similar purposes. That is all that the Court's test, which allows and even encourages "analogical reasoning," purports to require. . . .

In each instance, the Court finds a reason to discount the historical evidence's persuasive force. Some of the laws New York has identified are too old. But others are too recent. Still others did not last long enough. Some applied to too few people. Some were enacted for the wrong reasons. Some may have been based on a constitutional rationale that is now impossible to identify. Some arose in historically unique circumstances. And some are not sufficiently analogous to the licensing regime at issue here. But if the examples discussed above, taken together, do not show a tradition and history of regulation that supports the validity of New York's law, what could? Sadly, I do not know the answer to that question. What is worse, the Court appears to have no answer either.

V

. . . New York's Legislature considered the empirical evidence about gun violence and adopted a reasonable licensing law to regulate the concealed carriage of handguns in order to keep the people of New York safe. The Court today strikes down that law based only on the pleadings. It gives the State no opportunity to present evidence justifying its reasons for adopting the law or showing how the law actually operates in practice, and it does not so much as acknowledge these important considerations. Because I cannot agree with the Court's decision to strike New York's law down without allowing for discovery or the development of any evidentiary record, without considering the State's compelling interest in preventing gun violence and protecting the safety of its citizens, and without considering the potentially deadly consequences of its decision, I respectfully dissent.

Discussion

1. *Text, history and tradition. Bruen* exemplifies how the Court's conservative Justices have tended to merge originalist arguments with arguments from tradition.

Original meaning and tradition are not the same thing. Originalists generally look to the meaning or understanding of texts at the time of adoption. A focus on tradition is a bit different: instead of looking at meanings or understandings, it looks at the continuity of practices over long periods of time. Traditions do not have to begin at any particular point in time and they may change over time. For example, if a right was not recognized at the Founding but there is a long tradition of protecting it that developed in the 1880s, there would not be an originalist argument for the right but it there would be an argument from tradition.

Thomas's text and history test tends to merge considerations of original meaning and tradition. He argues that people have a presumptive right to engage in conduct covered by the amendment's text. Government may only regulate this conduct if there is a historical tradition of regulating it. By "this Nation's historical tradition of firearm regulation," he means a tradition of firearm regulation existing at the time of the adoption of the Second Amendment — or possibly at the time of adoption of the Fourteenth Amendment, which applies the Amendment to the States. Thomas's opinion does not decide whether we look to the tradition of regulation as of 1791 or 1868. Instead, his opinion runs these two periods together, assuming that they constitute a single unbroken tradition. What should the Court do if the tradition of regulation is different in the two eras?

2. *The problem with tradition.* Tests based on tradition tend to have three problems. The first is that arguments about tradition are told from the perspective of the present, and necessarily involve stories we tell ourselves about what the past must have been like. But because human behavior over a wide range of places and times may not actually fit neatly into a simple cohesive narrative, courts must tell a story that overlooks or excludes certain features of the past as not counting or as exceptions. (Thomas does this, for example, with Texas's nineteenth century regulations).

Second, arguments for following tradition assume that the tradition is wise or morally worthy from today's perspective. But if the tradition is outmoded, premised on facts that no longer hold true today, or reflects immoral or unjust practices, it is not clear why we should follow the tradition today. So, for example, the practices of gun regulation in the late eighteenth century assumed weapons that were far less powerful, agile, and effective than today's guns, operating in much less densely populated areas. They may also have reflected different moral assumptions about violence.

Third, if we are using tradition only as evidence of original meaning, it is not enough to show that a practice existed. One must also show that people self-consciously understood the practice — which might be quite different in diverse contexts and places — to be part of the meaning of the text that they adopted. In the case of firearm regulation, this may be very difficult to do.

3. *A theory of constitutional rights.* Thomas argues that his text and history approach to Second Amendment rights "accords with how we protect other constitutional rights." But it is very hard to credit this, especially in areas like the First Amendment's Free Speech Clause or the Equal Protection Clause. These clauses are governed for the most part by various tests of scrutiny.

Thomas argues that the substantive content of a constitutional right is determined by its scope at the time of adoption. Under this approach, for example, the substantive content of the Equal Protection Clause (for example) would be determined by the kinds of laws and practices in place in 1868. Given what you have learned so far in this course, do you agree that this is how the Court interprets the Constitution generally?

4. *One step, not two.* As Justice Thomas notes, the courts of appeals had converged on a two-step test which the Court rejects. The first step asked whether the regulated activity was even within the scope of the Second Amendment at the time of adoption. If not, then the regulation is upheld. If the activity is within the scope of the right, or the question is uncertain, the second step applies intermediate scrutiny (or strict scrutiny if the regulation strikes at the core right to possess guns for self-defense in the home.) Note that the two-step test gives the government two ways to win. The government can show that the activity in question was not protected (or was regulated) at the time of adoption, or the government can show that its regulation passes judicial scrutiny.

Thomas rejects this test, presumably because it allows too much regulation. His new "one-step" test presumes that government may not regulate activity described by the text (i.e., keeping and bearing arms) unless there is an adoption-era tradition of regulating it. This places the burden of proof on the government, making it easier for the government to lose.

5. *The* Heller *caveat.* Justice Kavanaugh's concurrence recites two paragraphs and a footnote from *Heller* and *McDonald* that list a set of "longstanding" firearm regulations that are deemed constitutional. These include restrictions on felons, the mentally ill, on carrying guns in "sensitive places," and "laws imposing conditions and qualifications on the commercial sale of arms." As Justice Breyer points out in dissent, several of these regulations did not exist at the time of adoption. They make sense from the standpoint of following tradition, but not necessarily from the standpoint of following the original meaning. Once again, the Court's opinion tends to run the two together.

6. *History, not scrutiny rules.* Justice Thomas argues that his historical approach is superior to using levels of scrutiny—as courts do, for example, in equal protection doctrine. Scrutiny rules empower judges to uphold regulations based on their case-by-case assessment of the utility of a particular regulation and the benefits and dangers to the public. Thomas argues that this approach makes it too easy for judges to defer to legislatures, and it gives them too much power to read their personal judgments into the law. Instead, "reliance on history to inform the meaning of constitutional text . . . is, in our view, more legitimate, and more administrable, than asking judges to 'make difficult empirical

judgments' about 'the costs and benefits of firearms restrictions,' especially given their 'lack [of] expertise' in the field."

One might respond that judges are no better at being professional historians, and that they are likely to view history selectively to read their personal judgments into law. (Compare Justice Thomas's and Justice Breyer's dueling accounts of history in this case.)

Why are judicial inquiries into the details of early historical practice better able to resolve questions of contemporary liberty and public safety than debates about the real-world effects of guns and gun regulations in the present? Thomas responds that the Framers already struck a balance between liberty and safety. But if their command is ambiguous or unclear, why should contemporary judges reject contemporary factual evidence? Put another way, why doesn't the Constitution's own language — which announces an abstract right — delegate to current generations the task of figuring out how best to secure the right to keep and bear arms in contemporary circumstances?

Thomas's response is that the balance between liberty and safety "struck by the traditions of the American people . . . demands our unqualified deference." That is, the meaning of the Amendment incorporates the balancing done by Founding-era (or Reconstruction-era) legislatures. But as cities have gotten larger and more densely populated, more powerful and accurate kinds of weapons have been invented, and social contexts have changed, legislatures have continued to try to balance liberty and safety. Why should the early legislative attempts at balancing liberty and safety in very different social and technological contexts be baked into the meaning of the Amendment today?

7. *Judges as historians.* Thomas concedes that judges cannot do comprehensive historical research themselves. This may be especially problematic for lower court judges, who, unlike the Supreme Court, cannot control the size of their own docket and have fewer clerks. Justice Thomas argues that this is not a problem, because judges will rely on the briefs of counsel and amici. Do we have reason to believe that counsel and amici will not read history selectively? After all, lawyers make arguments to win cases for their clients and for the causes they represent.

Can we rely on competition between the two sides of a lawsuit to give judges a sufficiently comprehensive and objective view of the historical materials? What features of history are likely to be left out of briefs by competing litigants? Will judges be tempted to pay more attention to evidence from counsel and amici they trust (because of ideological sympathies, for example), while discounting contrary evidence from the other side?

8. *Analogy, not scrutiny rules.* Justice Thomas acknowledges that contemporary legislatures responding to contemporary problems may pass laws that may not be identical to those existing at the time of adoption. For this reason, he explains that judges will sometimes have to reason by analogy to decide whether today's regulations are sufficiently similar to regulations in the past. He suggests that the central question is "whether modern and historical regulations impose a

comparable burden on the right of armed self-defense and whether that burden is comparably justified" But what is "comparable" and "comparably justified" may look different to a person generally skeptical of gun regulation and a person who believes guns pose a significant threat to public safety. One might also want to take into account differences in the destructive power and reloading speed of modern weapons, as well as the far more densely packed environment of contemporary American cities. How successful do you think Thomas's embrace of analogical reasoning will be in cabining judicial discretion or preventing judges from reading their ideological priors into the law?

9. *Precedent and bad history.* Suppose that the Supreme Court (or a circuit court) reaches a historical conclusion that is later discovered to be incorrect in the view of professional historians and historical linguists. May a later court reject the earlier historical conclusion, it or is it "baked-in" as precedent that lower courts must accept as historically correct? (Note, for example, that although Justice Breyer believes that *Heller*'s historical analysis is dubious, he accepts *Heller* as precedent.) Why should courts' historical conclusions be subject to stare decisis? On the other hand, if earlier courts' historical conclusions can be revisited, won't that make precedents insecure?

10. *May issue and shall issue.* As Justice Breyer points out, there is a spectrum of different positions between "may issue" and "shall issue" jurisdictions. For Justice Thomas, what matters constitutionally is that legislation employ "'narrow, objective, and definite standards' guiding licensing officials, rather than requiring the 'appraisal of facts, the exercise of judgment, and the formation of an opinion.'" Why should objective standards not require appraisal of facts?

Suppose a jurisdiction has objective standards but they are burdensome. For example, suppose instead of requiring a short (say 15 hour) course on gun safety as some jurisdictions do before granting a license, they require a 50 hour course, as well as ten signed character references and proof of a certain level of target accuracy? How should courts assess these questions?

11. *Sensitive places.* Justice Thomas follows the *Heller* caveat when he notes that legislatures may regulate the presence of guns in "sensitive places," but he rejects New York's claim that the entire island of Manhattan is such a place. What is a "sensitive place" in twenty-first-century America? What kind of showing must a government make?

In response to *Bruen*, New York state quickly passed a new gun control law. See Reuters, Factbox: What's in New York's new gun laws after Supreme Court ruling?, Reuters, July 1, 2022, https://www.reuters.com/world/us/whats-new -yorks-new-gun-laws-after-supreme-court-ruling-2022-07-02/. The new law defines as sensitive places government buildings, medical facilities, places of worship, libraries, playgrounds, parks, zoos, schools, summer camps, addiction-support centers, homeless shelters, nursing homes, public transit including the New York City subway, places where alcohol or marijuana is consumed, museums, theaters, stadiums, polling places and New York City's Times Square. It also provides, as a default rule, that guns are not allowed in private businesses unless the owner allows it. Are any or all of these restrictions constitutional under *Bruen*?

12. *Weapons in common use.* Justice Thomas also follows *Heller* in noting that the Amendment protects only weapons in "common use" today. How do we tell if a weapon is in common use? Consider the AR-15 semiautomatic rifle used in several recent mass shootings. The 1994 Federal Assault Weapon Ban signed into law by President Clinton banned certain models of the AR-15, but it did not ban all semi-automatic weapons and had many loopholes. The law expired in 2004, and since then the AR-15 has become one of the country's most popular weapons. See Jon Schuppe, America's Rifle: Why So Many People Love the AR-15, NBC News, December 27, 2017, https://www.nbcnews.com/news/us-news/america-s-rifle-why-so-many-people-love-ar-15-n831171.

If a weapon is owned by many people, is it irrelevant how powerful it is? Conversely, if a weapon can allow a person to cause a great deal of damage, is it irrelevant how many people own one? Or do we balance these considerations (and possibly others as well)? For discussions of regulations of semi-automatic rifles in the lower courts, see Kolbe v. Hogan, 849 F.3d 114 (4th Cir. 2017); Heller v. District of Columbia (*Heller II*) 670 F.3d 1244 (D.C. Cir. 2011); *id.* at 1288-1291 (Kanvanaugh, J., dissenting).

13. *New regulations.* How will *Bruen*'s test apply to new kinds of regulations that have no obvious analogue in the Founding era? For example, "red flag" laws permit police to petition a state or local court to order the temporary removal of firearms from a person who they believe may present a danger to others or themselves. Some states may impose limits on persons who have engaged in domestic abuse (but who are not convicted felons). Others may impose age limits on certain types of guns but not others.

Some of these laws may fall within the *Heller* caveat. But if not, then one must search for historical analogies at the Founding (or Reconstruction). If none exist, then legislatures cannot use these devices to protect public safety. Justice Kavanaugh's concurrence, joined by Chief Justice Roberts, is written to assuage concerns on this score and to suggest that the Justices will not strike down sensible regulations. But it is not clear how the Court's new historical test interacts with these assurances. Moreover, most constitutional challenges will not be decided by the Supreme Court. They will be decided by lower courts, who must analyze the new test of *Bruen* and apply it to a range of novel regulations.